FITTING

WORDS

Answer Key

FITTING WORDS

CLASSICAL RHETORIC

Answer Key

ROMAN
ROADS
MEDIA

In this series:

Resource
Fitting Words Textbook
Fitting Words Student Workbook
Fitting Words Answer Key (this book)
Fitting Words Exam Pack
Fitting Words Video Course

Fitting Words Answer Key

Second Edition (Version 2.0.0)

Copyright © 2018 by Roman Roads Media, LLC
Copyright © 2016 by Roman Roads Media, LLC

Published by Roman Roads Media
Moscow, Idaho
www.romanroadsmedia.com

Cover design concept by Rachel Rosales (Organe Peal Design).
Interior illustration by George Harrell. Interior design by Valerie Anne Bost.

ISBN-13: 978-1-944482-31-2
ISBN-10: 1-944482-31-8

TABLE OF CONTENTS

LESSON EXERCISES

 # COMPONENTS OF THIS COURSE

F*itting Words: Classical Rhetoric for the Christian Student* is meant as a one-year course in practical rhetoric for the Christian high school student. The entire packet includes these components:

1. The **textbook** with thirty lessons on the art of rhetoric. Each lesson also includes Thinking Deeper questions, suggestions for Reading Further, and quotes for Developing Memory. The Thinking Deeper sections provide optional questions for discussion, questions which dig further into the lesson topics. These occasionally require outside reading. The Developing Memory sections give the students exercise in memorizing and delivering appropriate quotes of varying length. Before starting this course you may find it helpful to read Lesson 29, which discusses some methods for memorizing. Students will write and deliver speeches after Lessons 13, 14, 15, 16, and 30. The appendices include a glossary of key terms, the text of the primary speeches used throughout the course, and a chart of every speech in the Bible, many of which are also used throughout the course.

2. The **student workbook**, which includes exercises for each lesson. Many of the lessons have two exercises, A and B, both of which should be completed by the student before going on to the next lesson. Also included are speech judging sheets identical to those in the test packet, which the student may use to evaluate himself as he practices the required speeches.

3. An **answer key** for the exercises and the tests. Also included is a proposed course schedule. The answer key layout matches the layout of the exercises and tests for ease of grading. Point suggestions are given [in brackets] for the exams only.

4. The **exam packet**, which includes review sheets for the tests, the tests themselves, and speech judging sheets for the instructor to evaluate the speeches to be delivered by the student. The final evaluation for the course is not a comprehensive exam but a final speech. Review sheets, tests, and judging

sheets are items which may be individually copied and distributed to the students at various times throughout the course.

5. In the **video course** that accompanies this text, each lesson is introduced and taught through two videos: a main lesson video which walks you through the lesson from the textbook, and a seperate application video which walks students through the exercises. Each lesson also introduces a figure of speech or thought (retaught together in Lessons 27 and 28), and suggestions for the optional Thinking Deeper discussions. The video also includes 9 exam prep videos.

# OPTIONAL COURSE SCHEDULES

Below are suggested schedules for teaching the *Fitting Words* course over one or two years. The one-year schedule shows four class meetings per week. Classes that meet five times per week can use the additional time to discuss the Thinking Deeper questions. Of course these are merely suggestions to help you to pace the lessons; you will know best what works for you and your students.

ONE-YEAR SCHEDULE: SEMESTER ONE

WEEK	DAY	TEXT AND ASSIGNMENT
Unit 1: Foundations of Rhetoric		
1	1	Preface: How to Use This Book Introduction: The Goal and Purpose of This Book
	2	Read Appendix A: Speeches
	3	Lesson 1: A Christian View of Rhetoric
	4	Exercise 1
2	5	Lesson 2: The Birth of Rhetoric
	6	Exercise 2
	7	Lesson 3: First Excerpt of Phaedrus
	8	Exercise 3
3	9	Lesson 4: Second Excerpt of Phaedrus
	10	Exercise 4
	11	Review for exam
	12	Exam 1
Unit 2: Invention and Arrangement		
4	13	Lesson 5: The Five Faculties of Oratory; Invention
	14	Exercise 5
	15	Finish exercise 5
	16	Lesson 6: Arrangement: Introduction
5	17	Exercise 6
	18	Finish exercise 6
	19	Lesson 7: Arrangement: Narration and Division
	20	Exercise 7
6	21	Finish exercise 7
	22	Lesson 8: Arrangement: Proof and Refutation
	23	Exercise 8
	24	Finish exercise 8
7	25	Lesson 9: Arrangement: Conclusion
	26	Exercise 9
	27	Review for exam
	28	Exam 2
Unit 3: Understanding Emotions: Ethos and Pathos		
8	29	Lesson 10: Ethos and Copiousness
	30	Exercise 10
	31	Finish exercise 10

WEEK	DAY	TEXT AND ASSIGNMENT
Unit 3 (continued)		
	32	Lesson 11: Pathos
9	33	Exercise 11
	34	Finish exercise 11
	35	Lesson 12: Emotions, Part One
	36	Exercise 12
10	37	Finish exercise 12
	38	Lesson 13: Emotions, Part Two
	39	Exercise 13
	40	Finish exercise 13
11	41	Speech prep
	42	Deliver Emotions speech
	43	Review for exam
	44	Exam 3
Unit 4: Fitting Words to the Topic: Special Lines of Argument		
12	45	Lesson 14: Special Lines of Argument: Forensic Oratory
	46	Exercise 14a
	47	Exercise 14b
	48	Speech prep
13	49	Speech prep
	50	Deliver Forensic speech
	51	Lesson 15: Political Oratory
	52	Exercise 15a
14	53	Exercise 15b
	54	Speech prep
	55	Speech prep
	56	Deliver Political speech
15	57	Lesson 16: Ceremonial Oratory
	58	Exercise 16a
	59	Exercise 16b
	60	Speech prep
16	61	Speech prep
	62	Deliver Ceremonial speech
	63	Review for exam
	64	Exam 4

ONE-YEAR SCHEDULE: SEMESTER TWO

WEEK	DAY	TEXT AND ASSIGNMENT

Unit 5: General Lines of Argument

WEEK	DAY	TEXT AND ASSIGNMENT
1	65	Lesson 17: General Lines of Argument; Terms and Definition
	66	Exercise 17a
	67	Exercise 17b
	68	Finish exercise 17b
2	69	Lesson 18: Statement Types and Their Relationships
	70	Exercise 18a
	71	Exercise 18b
	72	Finish exercise 18b
3	73	Lesson 19: Statements and Truth
	74	Exercise 19a
	75	Exercise 19b
	76	Finish exercise 19b
4	77	Lesson 20: Maxims and Their Use
	78	Exercise 20
	79	Review for exam
	80	Exam 5
5	81	Lesson 21: Argument by Example
	82	Exercise 21a
	83	Exercise 21b
	84	Finish exercise 21b
6	85	Lesson 22: Deductive Arguments
	86	Exercise 22a
	87	Exercise 22b
	88	Finish exercise 22b
7	89	Review for exam
	90	Exam 6
	91	Lesson 23: Refutation of Arguments
	92	Exercise 23a
8	93	Exercise 23b
	94	Finish exercise 23b
	95	Lesson 24: Informal Fallacies
	96	Exercise 24a
9	97	Finish exercise 24a
	98	Exercise 24b
	99	Review for exam
	100	Exam 7

Unit 6: Fitting Words to the Audience: Style and Ornament

WEEK	DAY	TEXT AND ASSIGNMENT
10	101	Lesson 25: Understanding Your Audience
	102	Exercise 25a
	103	Finish exercise 25a
	104	Exercise 25b
11	105	Lesson 26: Style: Clarity and Elegance
	106	Exercise 26a
	107	Finish exercise 26a
	108	Exercise 26b
12	109	Lesson 27: Levels of Style and Figures of Speech
	110	Exercise 27a
	111	Finish exercise 27a
	112	Exercise 27b
13	113	Finish exercise 27b
	114	Lesson 28: Tropes and Allusions
	115	Exercise 28a
	116	Finish exercise 28a
14	117	Exercise 28b
	118	Finish exercise 28b
	119	Review for exam
	120	Exam 8

Unit 7: Memory and Delivery

WEEK	DAY	TEXT AND ASSIGNMENT
15	121	Lesson 29: Memory
	122	Exercise 29
	123	Lesson 30: Delivery
	124	Exercise 30a
16	125	Exercise 30b
	126	Review for exam
	127	Exam 9
	128	Speech prep
17	129	Speech prep
	130	Speech prep
	131	Speech prep
	132	Deliver Final speech

TWO-YEAR SCHEDULE

YEAR ONE

WEEK TEXT AND ASSIGNMENT

Unit 1: Foundations of Rhetoric
1   Introduction; Read Appendix A
2   Lesson 1: A Christian View of Rhetoric; Exercise 1
3   Lesson 2: The Birth of Rhetoric; Exercise 2
4   Lesson 3: First Excerpt of Phaedrus; Exercise 3
5   Lesson 4: Second Excerpt of Phaedrus; Exercise 4
6   Review for exam; Exam 1

Unit 2: Invention and Arrangement
7   Lesson 5: The Five Faculties of Oratory; Invention; Exercise 5
8   Lesson 6: Arrangement: Overview; Introduction; Exercise 6
9   Lesson 7: Arrangement: Narration and Division; Exercise 7
10 Lesson 8: Arrangement: Proof and Refutation; Exercise 8
11 Lesson 9: Arrangement: Conclusion; Exercise 9
12 Review for exam; Exam 2

Unit 3: Understanding Emotions: Ethos and Pathos
13 Lesson 10: Ethos and Copiousness; Exercise 10
14 Lesson 11: Pathos; Exercise 11
15 Lesson 12: Emotions, Part One; Exercise 12
16 Lesson 13: Emotions, Part Two; Exercise 13
17 Speech prep
18 Deliver emotions speech
19 Review for exam; Exam 3

Unit 4: Fitting Words to the Topic: Special Lines of Argument
20 Lesson 14: Special Lines of Argument: Forensic Oratory; Exercise 14a
21 Exercise 14b
22 Speech prep
23 Deliver forensic speech
24 Lesson 15: Political Oratory; Exercise 15a
25 Exercise 15b
26 Speech prep
27 Deliver political speech
28 Lesson 16: Ceremonial Oratory; Exercise 16a
29 Exercise 16b
30 Speech prep
31 Deliver ceremonial speech
32 Review for exam; Exam 4

YEAR TWO

WEEK TEXT AND ASSIGNMENT

Unit 5: General Lines of Argument
1   Lesson 17: General Lines of Argument; Terms and Definition; Exercise 17a
2   Exercise 17b
3   Lesson 18: Statement Types and Their Relationships; Exercise 18a
4   Exercise 18b
5   Lesson 19: Statements and Truth; Exercise 19a
6   Exercise 19b
7   Lesson 20: Maxims and Their Use; Exercise 20
8   Review for exam; Exam 5
9   Lesson 21: Argument by Example; Exercise 21a
10 Exercise 21b
11 Lesson 22: Deductive Arguments; Exercise 22a
12 Exercise 22b
13 Review for exam; Exam 6
14 Lesson 23: Refutation of Arguments; Exercise 23a
15 Exercise 23b
16 Lesson 24: Informal Fallacies; Exercise 24a
17 Exercise 24b
18 Review for exam; Exam 7

Unit 6: Fitting Words to the Audience: Style and Ornament
19 Lesson 25: Understanding Your Audience; Exercise 25a
20 Exercise 25b
21 Lesson 26: Style: Clarity and Elegance; Exercise 26a
22 Exercise 26b
23 Lesson 27: Levels of Style and Figures of Speech; Exercise 27a
24 Exercise 27b
25 Lesson 28: Tropes and Allusions; Exercise 28a
26 Exercise 28b
27 Review for exam; Exam 8

Unit 7: Memory and Delivery
28 Lesson 29: Memory; Exercise 29
29 Lesson 30: Delivery; Exercise 30a
30 Exercise 30b; Review for exam; Exam 9
31 Speech prep
32 Deliver Final speech

EXERCISE 1

1. Name and explain three distinct things a speaker can do to make his speech *in*effective. Find three passages not referenced in the lesson where the Bible speaks about how we should speak: one from Proverbs, one from Jesus in the Gospels, and a third from elsewhere in the New Testament. Draw one practical application for rhetoric from each.

   First, a speaker could mumble his way through his speech with a lot of "um" and "you know" instead of being articulate. Second, he could reveal a lack of knowledge about his subject or be ignorant of his opponent's arguments. Third, he could project a lack of interest in or conviction about his subject, speaking in a monotone voice or making no eye contact, and so hinder the audience from being interested in what he has to say.

2. Find three passages not referenced in the lesson where the Bible speaks about how we should speak: one from Proverbs, one from Jesus in the gospels, and a third from elsewhere in the New Testament. Draw one practical application for rhetoric from each.

   Proverbs 15:1—"A soft answer turns away wrath, but a harsh word stirs up anger." From this we learn that the tone of our voice can affect the emotions of our hearers. (See also Prov. 12:18, 13:3, 18:21, 26:4–5.)
   Matthew 13:19–23—Jesus interprets the Parable of the Sower. He teaches that the same message can produces different

1

responses in different people depending on their circumstances and heart condition. What persuades one person will not persuade all. (See also Matt. 18:15–17, John 5:30–47.)
Ephesians 4:11–15—Paul teaches that God gave different speaking gifts (apostles, prophets, evangelists, pastors and teachers) to build up and unite the church, and protect it from false teaching. Verse 15 says we are to speak the truth in love. (See also Acts 4:13, 4:29–31, 18:24–28.)

EXERCISE 2

NAME

DATE

Consider this structural analysis of an excerpt from Gorgias's *Encomium of Helen*. Note that parallel (meaning similar or opposite) words or phrases are placed one above the other.

> In many did she work desire for her love, and
> her one body was the cause of bringing together
>   many bodies of men
>   thinking great thoughts for
>   great goals,
>   of whom some had greatness of wealth,
>   some the glory of ancient nobility,
>   some the vigor of personal agility,
>   some the command of acquired knowledge.
> And all came because of a passion which loved to conquer and
>   a love of honor which was unconquered.

Arrange the following brief speeches from the Old Testament using this same method.

1. Ruth 1:16–17

> Entreat me not to leave you, or
>   to turn back from following after you;
> For wherever you go,
>   I will go; and
>   wherever you lodge,
>   I will lodge;
>   Your people shall be
>   my people, and
>   your God,
>   my God.

Where you die,

      I will die, and

   there will I be buried.

The LORD do so to me, and

         more also,

If anything but death parts you and me.

2. 1 Samuel 17:45–47

You come to me with a sword,

         with a spear, and

         with a javelin.

But I come to you in the name of the LORD of hosts,

         the God of the armies of Israel,

         whom you have defied.

This day the LORD will deliver you into my hand, and

     I will strike you and

       take your head from you. And

this day I will give the carcasses of the camp of the Philistines

       to the birds of the air and

       the wild beasts of the earth,

that all the earth may know that there is a God in Israel.

Then all this assembly shall know that the LORD does not save

with sword and spear;

for the battle is the LORD's, and

   He will give you into our hands.

EXERCISE 3

1. What is the first thing that Socrates says a good speaker must know? Contrary to this, what has Phaedrus heard to be the source of persuasion for orators? [259–260]

   <u>Socrates implies that the speaker must know the truth of the</u>
   <u>matter about which he is going to speak. Phaedrus has heard</u>
   <u>that opinion, rather than truth, produces persuasion.</u>

2. What does Lady Rhetoric claim that she is able to give? What does she not claim to give?

   <u>She claims to give the art of persuasion, but not the</u>
   <u>knowledge of the truth. Those who would speak should arrive</u>
   <u>at the truth first and then come to her.</u>

3. Phaedrus says that the practice of rhetoric has been confined to courts of law and public assemblies. In the lines prior, what does Socrates imply that its scope should be? [261]

   <u>Socrates implies that the scope of rhetoric should be universal,</u>
   <u>"practiced not only in courts and public assemblies, but in</u>
   <u>private houses also, having to do with all matters."</u>

4. What does Socrates criticize the professors of the art of rhetoric (he has in mind the sophists) for doing?

Socrates says that they speak on opposite sides of the issue as it pleases them, rather than speaking only truth. They make the same thing appear to the same persons to be at one time just and at another time to be unjust, or good and the reverse of good.

5. Socrates claims that "he who would be a master of the art must understand the real nature of everything." Explain why (there are a couple of reasons). [262]

Socrates claims that rhetoricians must understand the real nature of everything so that they can deceive others by gradually departing from truth into error and so that they can avoid being so deceived themselves.

6. Having listened to the first few lines of Lysias's speech, what two suggestions does Socrates make for the rhetorician (what ought he to do, and what must he observe)? What does he further imply that a rhetorician should do (that Lysias did not do)? [263]

Socrates says that the rhetorician ought to distinguish between the certain and the uncertain classes of things (things people agree about and disagree about). Also, the rhetorician must observe the particulars of the subject he is speaking on. Third, he implies that a rhetorician should define his key terms.

_____

_____

_____

7. Having heard the first few lines of Lysias's speech for a second time, what further suggestion does Socrates make regarding the practice of rhetoric? [264]

    Socrates argues that a rhetorician must arrange the parts of his speech in an orderly, principled manner, with a beginning, middle, and end adapted to one another and to the whole.

    _____

    _____

8. What additional two principles must rhetoricians follow, according to Socrates? [265–266]

    The first principle is that the rhetorician must comprehend the scattered particulars of his subject in one well-defined idea, giving them clarity and consistency.
    The second principle is that of dividing the subject into species in a natural way so that the divisions are seen to be balanced and complete.
    These two methods Socrates calls generalization and division, the one and the many.

    _____

    _____

    _____

    _____

EXERCISE 4

NAME

DATE

1. List in order the parts of a discourse noted by Socrates (there are about eight of them) that were to be found in the handbooks of rhetoric. [266–267]

   <u>The exordium, statement of facts, witnesses, proofs,</u>
   <u>probabilities, confirmation, refutation, and recapitulation or</u>
   <u>summing up. (Other devices are mentioned, such as diplasiology</u>
   <u>and gnomology, but these are not presented as parts of a</u>
   <u>discourse.)</u>

2. Socrates makes an analogy between the rhetoricians of his day and those who would misuse the arts of medicine, tragedy, and music. Explain the analogy, and summarize his related criticism of rhetoric. [268–269, 272]

   <u>Socrates says that someone who knows just the preliminaries</u>
   <u>of medicine (how to apply certain drugs), or of tragedy (how</u>
   <u>to make different kinds of speeches), or of music (how to pitch</u>
   <u>the highest and lowest notes), but does not fully understand</u>
   <u>these arts and their proper application, is like one who knows</u>
   <u>only the preliminaries of rhetoric (such as the parts of speech</u>
   <u>and other devices), but considers himself a master rhetorician.</u>
   <u>Those who teach rhetoric students only the preliminaries of</u>
   <u>rhetoric, but do not teach how to apply them, thinking that</u>
   <u>the students can figure this out for themselves, do not really</u>
   <u>teach the full art of rhetoric.</u>

3. According to Socrates, what the three things must one have to be "a distinguished speaker"? [269]

<u>To be a distinguished speaker, one must have natural power,</u>
<u>knowledge, and practice.</u>

4. What must a true rhetorician know about the soul? Explain what this means. [271–272]

<u>Socrates says that oratory is the art of enchanting the soul,</u>
<u>so the true rhetorician first must describe the nature of the</u>
<u>soul, whether it is single or multiform. Second, he must explain</u>
<u>the mode in which the soul acts or is acted upon. Third, he</u>
<u>must show why one soul is persuaded by a particular form of</u>
<u>argument, and another not.</u>
<u>By the "soul" he means the person, as he makes clear when</u>
<u>he says that from the differences of human souls come the</u>
<u>differences between man and man. This means the rhetorician</u>
<u>must learn the differences of human personalities and, after</u>
<u>dividing speeches into different classes, explain why different</u>
<u>types of people are affected by different classes of speech. He</u>
<u>must know these things theoretically and experientially.</u>

5. Summarize the method of basing argument on probability. How does this method go astray, according to Socrates? [272–273]

> An argument of probability is an argument based on likelihood, i.e., what is most probable under the circumstances, or what most people would think to be the case if they did not know the facts. This method goes astray when the speaker considers only probability and ignores the truth. This is, in fact, what many people do: in trying to be convincing they ignore the actual facts.

6. Socrates summarizes his suggestions for developing rhetoric as a true art. Rewrite three of these suggestions in a brief, coherent paragraph. [273–274, 277]

> A rhetorician who practices the true art of rhetoric must first understand the nature of the soul, i.e., the differences among his hearers' personalities, so that he can match the right kinds of speech with the right kind of hearers in order to persuade them. Second, he must be able to unite the scattered particulars of a topic under a single, clearly defined idea, and divide them again in a balanced and complete manner. Third, he must put forth the effort to do this not in order to please men, but to please God first.

EXERCISE 5

NAME

DATE

1. Write a thesis statement on a topic that interests you. Make sure that your statement is disputable, provable, clear, and interesting. This statement will be used in later exercises, as well.

   <u>Christians should learn propositional logic. (Sample Answer)</u>

2. For the thesis statement above, develop specific questions of stasis. Include at least two specific questions for each of the four categories. Then briefly answer the questions.

   Conjecture: <u>Do Christians learn propositional logic? Most</u>
   <u>classical Christian schools and homeschools usually teach some</u>
   <u>logic, but many do not include propositional logic.</u>
   <u>Who developed propositional logic? The Stoic philosopher</u>
   <u>Chrysippus was the first to develop a system of propositional</u>
   <u>logic, in the third century BC. It was first developed into</u>
   <u>symbolic form by Leibniz in the eighteenth century, and later</u>
   <u>by Russell, Whitehead, et al.</u>

Definition: <u>What kind of thing is propositional logic? Propositional logic is a branch of formal logic like categorical logic.</u>
<u>Is it properly called logic? Yes, because, like categorical logic, it deals with methods of analyzing arguments to determine their validity.</u>

Quality: <u>Is it expedient for Christians to study propositional logic? Yes, because propositional logic, being more flexible and powerful, can be used to analyze more actual arguments than categorical logic.</u>
<u>Is it honorable to study propositional logic? Though propositional logic (like categorical logic) was developed by unbelievers, this does not taint the student or bring him dishonor, since by God's common grace these unbelievers discovered true and helpful methods of understanding the language of arguments.</u>

Policy: <u>Should some action be taken? Courses that teach</u> <u>propositional logic from a Christian foundation should be</u> <u>offered.</u>
<u>Who should do it? Christian publishers should write textbooks</u> <u>that teach propositional logic, and Christian schools should</u> <u>offer classes that teach it.</u>

EXERCISE 6

NAME

DATE

1. Consider your thesis statement and answers to Exercise 5. Write a brief introduction for a speech on your topic from the first six types of introduction presented in this lesson, and identify which type(s) you use. You may invent a fictitious setting for the speech.

   Tertullian once famously asked, "What has Athens to do with Jerusalem?" Why should Christians, who have in the Bible all truth and wisdom, turn to modern propositional logic as an aid to gaining wisdom? Was not this modern system of logic developed by unbelieving philosophers from non-Christian assumptions? Why follow scientific modernity in its flight from traditional logic, a method of logic grounded in Christian truth and employed in its defense for centuries? (Types 3 and 6.) (Sample Answer)

2. Read this introduction of *Here I Stand*, in which Martin Luther defends himself before the Diet of Worms (an imperial deliberative body held in Worms, Germany, in 1521).

   Most Serene Emperor, and you illustrious princes and gracious lords: I this day appear before you in all humility, according to your command, and I implore Your Majesty and your august highnesses, by the mercies of God, to listen with favor to the defense of a cause which I am well assured is just

17

and right. I ask pardon, if by reason of my ignorance, I am wanting in the manners that befit a court; for I have not been brought up in kings' palaces, but in the seclusion of a cloister.

This introduction primarily refers to the occasion of the speech. Rewrite it with Luther asking questions, instead, including in them most of the same information.

Most Serene Emperor, and you illustrious princes and gracious lords: Why do I appear before you this day? Is it not according to your command? Will Your Majesty and your august highnesses listen to the defense of a cause which I am well assured is just and right? Or will you malign me because of my ignorance, my manners, and my upbringing, which has been not in kings' palaces, but in the seclusion of a cloister?

3. Read the introduction to Cicero's *First Oration Against Catiline*, delivered before the Roman Senate in 63 BC.

When, O Catiline, do you mean to cease abusing our patience? How long is that madness of yours still to mock us? When is there to be an end of that unbridled audacity of yours, swaggering about as it does now? Do not the nightly guards placed on the Palatine Hill—do not the watches posted throughout the city—does not the alarm of the people, and the union of all good men—does not the precaution taken of assembling the senate in this most defensible place—do not the looks and countenances of this venerable body here present, have any effect upon you? Do you not feel that your plans are detected? Do you not see that your conspiracy is already arrested and rendered powerless by the knowledge which every one here possesses of it? What is there that you did last night, what the night before—where is it that you were—who was there that you summoned to meet you—what design was there which was adopted by you, with which you think that any one of us is unacquainted?

This introduction directs rhetorical questions to the conspirator Catiline himself. Rewrite it by turning the questions into statements directed to the Senate. Include in it most of the same information.

O conscript fathers, Catiline has been abusing our patience. In his madness he is mocking us. There seems no end of his unbridled audacity, which swaggers about. Neither the nightly guards placed on the Palatine Hill, nor the watches posted throughout the city, nor the alarm of the people, nor the union of all good men, nor the precaution taken of assembling the senate in this most defensible place, nor the looks and countenances of this venerable body here present—none of these has any effect upon him. But he must feel that his plans are detected. He must see that his conspiracy is already arrested and rendered powerless by the knowledge which we all here possess of it. We are all of us acquainted with everything Catiline did last night and the night before: where he went, who was there that he summoned to meet him, even the design there which was adopted by him.

4. Consider your rewritten introductions from the previous two questions. How
   do the revised introductions affect the tone of each speech?

   Rewriting Martin Luther's introduction with rhetorical questions
   gives it a confrontational tone rather than the more humble
   and respectful tone of the original. On the contrary, changing
   Cicero's questions directed against Catiline into statements
   directed to the Senate removes much of the rhetorical force
   of the introduction, sapping it of its feeling of personal
   confrontation. Overall, both introductions appear weakened in
   emotional force.

EXERCISE 7

NAME

DATE

1. Consider Stephen's speech in Acts 7:2–53. Which verses constitute the narration? Defend your answer.

   The narration begins with historical background after an exhortation to listen in verse 2. The narration continues in like manner until verses 35–38, where Stephen gives a series of three parallel declarations: "This Moses is the one who . . ." but this is still statement of facts. The division appears to occupy verses 44–50, with a declaration of issues agreed upon and issues disputed. If so, the narration is from verse 2b through 43 (though one could argue that it continues through verse 47).

2. Considering the thesis statement and questions of stasis from Exercise 5, along with the introduction from Exercise 6, write a division for a speech on that topic. Include the points of agreement and contention, and a preview of the arguments.

   All Christian parents want their children to know how to learn something new, to understand the world around them, and to have insight into the character of its Creator. One way parents can help their sons and daughters along this educational path is to teach them propositional logic. Propositional (or symbolic) logic provides powerful methods by which students can learn how to learn, beyond the methods of traditional categorical logic. Tools

21

such as formal proofs of validity teach students how to reason in a straight line while providing them with standards and methods by which they can judge and correct their own arguments and analyze the arguments of others. The study of propositional logic can help them understand the history of thought while giving them insight into the modern digital age. Many Christian thinkers have found propositional logic to be interesting and valuable, and have contended that an enquiry into modern logic can aid us in understanding the nature and character of the God of the Bible. (Sample Answer)

EXERCISE 8

NAME

DATE

1. Read Acts 17:22–31. Most of Paul's speech (after verse 23) consists of proof. His thesis is in the second part of verse 29. Summarize four arguments of his proof, each written as an enthymeme (a statement with a supporting premise). Include verse numbers.

   Verse 24. God does not dwell in manmade temples, because He created all things and is Lord of both heaven and earth

   Verse 25. God does not need us nor our worship, because He sustains all life.

   Verses 26–27a. God has given men opportunity to seek Him, because He has made us and placed us in this world

   Verses 27b–28. God is not far from us, for in Him we live and move and have our being; we are His offspring.

   (The argument from verses 30–31 could be included.)

2. In the first two chapters of Romans, Paul argues that Jews and Gentiles are both alike under sin. Then in chapter three he presents a refutation section. Write out the first four objections—written as rhetorical questions—from Romans 3:1–9. (Note that some of the objections include two distinct questions, so the answer will comprise more than four questions.) Include the verse numbers.

   Verse 1. What advantage has the Jew? What is the profit of circumcision?

   Verse 3. What if some did not believe? Will their unbelief make the faithfulness of God without effect?

Verses 5–7. If our unrighteousness demonstrates the
righteousness of God, is God unjust to inflict wrath? If the
truth of God has increased through my lie to His glory, why
am I still judged as a sinner?

Verse 9. Are Jews any better than the Greeks?

EXERCISE 9

NAME

DATE

1. Woodrow Wilson's April 2, 1917, war speech, famous for declaring, "The world must be made safe for democracy," concludes with these two sentences:

> To such a task we can dedicate our lives and our fortunes, everything that we are and everything that we have, with the pride of those who know that the day has come when America is privileged to spend her blood and her might for the principles that gave her birth and happiness and the peace which she has treasured. God helping her, she can do no other.

Wilson here alludes to conclusions from two other famous speeches (both of which are included in Appendix A). Name them, and put the quotes from the originals next to the phrases from this conclusion for comparison.

Declaration of Independence: "we mutually pledge to each other our Lives, our Fortunes and our sacred Honor," "we can dedicate our lives and our fortunes..."

Martin Luther's Diet of Worms speech: "Here I stand; I cannot do otherwise. God help me," "God helping her, she can do no other."

Problems 2–10: Identify the type of conclusion used in each of these biblical speeches. The verses that make up the conclusion are identified in parentheses. (Hint: Each type is used at least once, none more than twice.)

2. Genesis 13:8–9 (9b) _contrast_

3. Genesis 44:18–34 (33–34) _summary_

4. Exodus 13:3–16 (16) _bookend (cf. v. 3)_

5. Deuteronomy 29:2—30:20 (30:19–20) _call to action_

6. Joshua 1:16–18 (18b) _famous saying (cf. Gen. 31:6, 23, Josh. 1:6)_

7. 1 Kings 18:9–14 (14) _bookend (cf. v. 8–9)_

8. 1 Chronicles 22:7–16 (16b) _call to action_

9. Matthew 10:5–42 (41–42) _prediction_

10. Acts 20:18–35 (35b) _famous saying_

EXERCISE 10

NAME

DATE

1. Which elements of ethos are mentioned by Christ when he sends out the twelve to preach (Matt. 10:16)? Explain your answer.

    <u>He mentions good sense ("Be as wise as serpents," calling</u>
    <u>them to be mentally sharp) and good moral character ("and as</u>
    <u>innocent as doves," calling them to be blameless).</u>

2. Read the introduction to Martin Luther's *Here I Stand* speech before the Diet of Worms. How does Luther establish each of the three parts of ethos? Defend your answers.

    > Most Serene Emperor, and you illustrious princes and gracious lords: I this day appear before you in all humility, according to your command, and I implore Your Majesty and your august highnesses, by the mercies of God, to listen with favor to the defense of a cause which I am well assured is just and right. I ask pardon, if by reason of my ignorance, I am wanting in the manners that befit a court; for I have not been brought up in kings' palaces, but in the seclusion of a cloister.

    <u>Good sense: Luther is prepared to defend himself with well-</u>
    <u>reasoned arguments.</u>
    <u>Good moral character: He is humble, obedient, and on the side</u>
    <u>of justice and righteousness.</u>
    <u>Good will toward hearers: He respects their social status, to</u>
    <u>the point of asking pardon for his rough manners.</u>

3. Read the excerpt from Letter from a Birmingham Jail. Where does Martin Luther King Jr. establish each of the three parts of ethos? Defend your answers.

My Dear Fellow Clergymen:

While confined here in the Birmingham city jail, I came across your recent statement calling my present activities "unwise and untimely." Seldom do I pause to answer criticism of my work and ideas. If I sought to answer all the criticisms that cross my desk, my secretaries would have little time for anything other than such correspondence in the course of the day, and I would have no time for constructive work. But since I feel that you are men of genuine good will and that your criticisms are sincerely set forth, I want to try to answer your statement in what I hope will be patient and reasonable terms.

I think I should indicate why I am here in Birmingham, since you have been influenced by the view which argues against "outsiders coming in." I have the honor of serving as president of the Southern Christian Leadership Conference, an organization operating in every southern state, with headquarters in Atlanta, Georgia. We have some eighty five affiliated organizations across the South, and one of them is the Alabama Christian Movement for Human Rights. Frequently we share staff, educational and financial resources with our affiliates. Several months ago the affiliate here in Birmingham asked us to be on call to engage in a nonviolent direct action program if such were deemed necessary. We readily consented, and when the hour came we lived up to our promise. So I, along with several members of my staff, am here because I was invited here. I am here because I have organizational ties here.

But more basically, I am in Birmingham because injustice is here. Just as the prophets of the eighth century B.C. left their villages and carried their "thus saith the Lord" far beyond the boundaries of their home towns, and just as the Apostle Paul left his village of Tarsus and carried the gospel of Jesus Christ to the far corners of the Greco Roman world, so am I compelled to carry the gospel of freedom beyond my own home town. Like Paul, I must constantly respond to the Macedonian call for aid.

Moreover, I am cognizant of the interrelatedness of all communities and states. I cannot sit idly by in Atlanta and not be concerned about what happens in Birmingham. Injustice anywhere is a threat to justice everywhere. We are caught in an inescapable network of mutuality, tied in a single garment of destiny.

Good sense: Dr. King says he want to answer them in "reasonable terms." He notes that he is president of "an organization operating in every southern state." He shows the clergymen that he is familiar with the Apostle Paul and his work. He understands the interrelatedness of people in different locations.

Good moral character: First, he opens with "fellow clergymen," including himself with his hearers in that honorable profession. He wants to devote his time to "constructive work." He argues that he has come to Birmingham not as an outside agitator, but because he was invited by an affiliate organization, is keeping a promise, and is seeking justice. In comparing himself to Paul, he presents himself as obedient to a call.

Good will toward hearers: He calls them "men of genuine good will," who by their sincerity show themselves worthy of a considered response. Finally, he shows that he is concerned about the people of Birmingham, as they should be.

EXERCISE 11

NAME

DATE

Problems 1–5: One indication that it is proper to appeal to emotions is the fact that the Bible often speaks of men whose hearts are hardened against feeling appropriate emotions. Look up the given verses and identify the emotion that hearts are hardened against. (It may help you to read the definitions of the various emotion in Lessons 12 and 13.)

1. Exodus 9:11–12 _shame_
2. Deuteronomy 2:26–30 _kindness_
3. Deuteronomy 15:7 _pity_
4. Proverbs 28:14 _fear_
5. Isaiah 63:17 _fear_

Problems 6–8: Read the refutation and conclusion of Patrick Henry's "Give Me Liberty" speech, and answer the related questions. (Line numbers have been added for convenience.)

[1]They tell us, sir, that we are weak—unable to cope with so formidable an adversary. [2]But when shall we be stronger? [3]Will it be the next week, or the next year? [4]Will it be when we are totally disarmed, and when a British guard shall be stationed in every house? [5]Shall we gather strength by irresolution and inaction? [6]Shall we acquire the means of effectual resistance by lying supinely on our backs and hugging the delusive phantom of hope, until our enemies shall have bound us hand and foot?

[7]Sir, we are not weak if we make a proper use of those means which the God of nature hath placed in our power. [8]Three millions of people, armed in the holy cause of liberty, and in such a country as that which we possess, are invincible by any force which our enemy can send against us. [9]Besides, sir, we shall not fight our battles alone. [10]There is a just God who presides over the destinies of nations, and who will raise up friends to fight our battles for us. [11]The battle, sir, is not to the strong alone; it is to the vigilant, the active, the brave. [12]Besides, sir, we have no election. [13]If we were base enough to desire it, it is now too late to retire from the contest. [14]There is

no retreat but in submission and slavery! ¹⁵Our chains are forged! ¹⁶Their clanking may be heard on the plains of Boston! ¹⁷The war is inevitable—and let it come! ¹⁸I repeat it, sir, let it come!

¹⁹It is in vain, sir, to extenuate the matter. ²⁰Gentlemen may cry, Peace, Peace—but there is no peace. ²¹The war is actually begun! ²²The next gale that sweeps from the north will bring to our ears the clash of resounding arms! ²³Our brethren are already in the field! ²⁴Why stand we here idle? ²⁵What is it that gentlemen wish? ²⁶What would they have? ²⁷Is life so dear, or peace so sweet, as to be purchased at the price of chains and slavery? ²⁸Forbid it, Almighty God! ²⁹I know not what course others may take; but as for me, give me liberty or give me death!

6. Describe the emotional impact of the rhetorical questions in the first and third paragraphs (lines 2–6 and 24–27). What emotion was Henry seeking to produce in his opponents (who opposed mobilizing for war)?

   His questions would make his opponents feel ashamed because they would presumably have no answer that would escape the force of his insinuations of them being indecisive and cowardly.

7. The rhetorical question in line 6 uses *enargia* to create a clear image in the minds of the audience. Rewrite it an as ordinary declarative sentence with no figurative language. How does this change affect the emotional impact?

   "We cannot acquire the means of effectual resistance by being submissive or seeking false hope until our enemies have overpowered us." This weakens the emotional impact of the vivid rhetorical question.

8. What emotion is he seeking to produce in the middle paragraph, especially
    lines 7–11? How do lines 17–18 and line 29 help to reinforce that emotion?

    Henry is trying to increase their confidence, to encourage
    them to fight, because they are stronger than they realize.
    He demonstrates the confidence and courage that he wants
    them to feel, though he knows that taking this stand could
    lead to his death.

EXERCISE 12

NAME

DATE

Problems 1–12: Identify the primary emotion from each lesson (anger, calmness, friendship, enmity, fear, confidence) that the given speaker is seeking to produce in his hearers.

1. Genesis 13:8–9 _friendship_

2. Exodus 14:13–14 _confidence_

3. Joshua 22:22–29 _calmness_

4. 1 Samuel 25:24–31 _calmness_

5. 1 Kings 1:17–21, 24–27 _anger_

6. 1 Kings 5:2–9 _friendship_

7. 2 Chronicles 13:4–7 _enmity_

8. Ezra 6:6–12 _fear_

9. Daniel 3:9–12 _anger_

10. Matthew 28:18–20 _confidence_

11. Mark 9:42–48 _fear_

12. Acts 24:5–8 _enmity_

13. Which emotion is Martin Luther trying to produce in the introduction to *Here I Stand?* Defend your answer.

> Most Serene Emperor, and you illustrious princes and gracious lords: I this day appear before you in all humility, according to your command, and I implore Your Majesty and your august highnesses, by the mercies of God, to listen with favor to the defense of a cause which I am well assured is just and right. I ask pardon, if by reason of my ignorance, I am wanting in the manners that befit a court; for I have not been brought up in kings' palaces, but in the seclusion of a cloister.

Luther is trying to produce calmness. The imperial audience
before whom he was defending himself may have included

35

many who were angry at him and who had the power to
punish him. Thus he is humble before them and speaks to them
respectfully.

Problems 14–15: Read the excerpt in Appendix A from Jonathan Edwards's sermon "Sinners in the Hand of an Angry God," and answer the following questions.

14. Explain how in his sermon Edwards employs each of the given elements of the definition of fear.

    pain or disturbance Edwards uses language that disturbs his
    hearers from their spiritual sloth.

    due to a mental picture He uses images of devouring flames;
    swords dangling overhead and pits underneath; being cut off,
    swallowed up, and lost.

    of destructive or painful evil He says that sin is "destructive in its
    nature" and calls hell "eternal destruction." He presents hell as
    painful, speaking of the "torments of hell."

    in the future He says "the pit is prepared, the fire is made
    ready, the furnace is now hot, ready to receive them . . . at
    what moment God shall permit."

15. Aristotle adds that "we know that we shall die, but we are not troubled thereby, because death is not close at hand." How does Edwards make death appear close at hand?

Edwards argues that death is close at hand to all of us, since God may bring an end to our life at any time. He argues that death is near in these ways: "It is no security to wicked men for one moment, that there are no visible means of death at hand ... this is no evidence, that a man is not on the very brink of eternity, and that the next step will not be into another world"; "God has so many different unsearchable ways of taking wicked men out of the world"; "men's own wisdom is no security to them from death." He also uses metaphors such as "unconverted men walk over the pit of hell on a rotten covering, and there are innumerable places in this covering so weak that they will not bear their weight, and these places are not seen. The arrows of death fly unseen at noonday; the sharpest sight cannot discern them."

EXERCISE 13

NAME

DATE

Problems 1–12: Identify the emotion(s) from this lesson (shame, kindness, pity, indignation, envy, emulation) that the given speaker was seeking to produce in his hearers.

1. Genesis 34:21–23 _envy / kindness_
2. Deuteronomy 32:10–15 _indignation_
3. Joshua 14:6–12 _kindness_
4. Judges 5:24–27 _emulation / shame_
5. Ruth 1:11–13 _pity_
6. 1 Samuel 26:15–16 _shame_
7. Nehemiah 2:5–8 _kindness_
8. Esther 8:5–6 _pity_
9. Proverbs 9:13–17 _envy_
10. Matthew 21:33–40 _indignation_
11. John 8:42–47 _shame_
12. 2 Timothy 4:6–8 _emulation_

Problems 13–15: The same speech may produce different emotions in different hearers. Read this excerpt from Martin Luther King Jr.'s speech *I Have a Dream*, and describe the type of hearer that would respond with the stated emotion. Explain your answer.

> Five score years ago, a great American, in whose symbolic shadow we stand today, signed the Emancipation Proclamation. This momentous decree came as a great beacon light of hope to millions of Negro slaves, who had been seared in the flames of withering injustice. It came as a joyous day-break to end the long night of their captivity. But one hundred years later, the Negro still is not free. One hundred years later, the life of the Negro is still sadly crippled by the manacles of segregation and the chains of discrimination. One hundred years later, the Negro lives on a lonely island of

poverty in the midst of a vast ocean of material prosperity. One hundred years later, the Negro still languishes in the corners of American society and finds himself an exile in his own land.

13. Pity

Pity would likely be felt by a hearer who had endured similar injustice but was no longer suffering in the same way. A compassionate person would especially feel pity if he or she were aware of others who were still suffering.

14. Shame

This speech would produce shame in a good-intentioned man who had the power to do something about the injustice described but had done nothing, especially if he had failed to deliver on any sincere and public promises to help right the wrongs.

15. Indignation

A hearer would be indignant toward the perpetrators of the injustice if he believed them to be doing nothing when it was in their power, especially if they were haughty and complacent. But if he was too close to the situation (suffering the same trials himself), anger could overwhelm indignation.

16. Select one of the emotions from Lesson 12 or 13, and write a portion of a speech seeking to produce that emotion in your hearers. Consider writing on the thesis you developed in Exercise 5. Identify at the end the intended emotion.

Many Christian thinkers and leaders have defended the study and use of modern symbolic logic. First among them is Vern S. Poythress, professor of New Testament interpretation at Westminster Theological Seminary and author of Logic: A God-Centered Approach to the Foundation of Western Thought. In this clearly written and comprehensive masterpiece, Poythress carefully explains how symbolic logic is founded in the nature and character of the true God of Scripture. Following years of study into the subject, Poythress has given us not just another logic textbook, but a revolutionary and distinctively Christian approach to logic in all of its major branches. Rarely has modern symbolic logic had such a God-honoring and able defender. Christians interested in modern logic would benefit from a careful reading not only of this book, but of those that Poythress himself studied to acquire his depth of knowledge and understanding.

Intended Emotion: _Emulation (Sample Answer)_

Read 2 Samuel, chapters 11 and 12, and answer the following questions.

1. Explain why Nathan's speech (2 Samuel 12:1–12) is an example of *forensic oratory* (consider the description of forensic oratory from the third paragraph of this lesson).

   <u>A forensic speech either accuses or defends someone based</u>
   <u>on the justice or injustice of his past actions. Nathan delivers</u>
   <u>a speech of accusation based on the injustice of David's past</u>
   <u>actions, proclaiming that David is guilty of wrongdoing.</u>

   _____

   _____

2. Of what two wrongs does Nathan accuse David? Choose one, and explain how it fits the elements of the definition of *wrongdoing*.

   <u>Nathan accuses David of committing adultery with Bathsheba</u>
   <u>and murdering her husband Uriah. Wrongdoing is injury,</u>
   <u>voluntarily inflicted, contrary to law. Murder obviously injures</u>
   <u>the victim (causing physical harm against his will); David's</u>
   <u>actions were voluntary (he sent a letter to have it carried</u>
   <u>out); and murder is contrary to all law. (Answer may vary.)</u>

   _____

   _____

   _____

3. Explain how David had the *opportunity* to commit adultery with Bathsheba.

   David had the chance to commit adultery at that place and
   time because he had sent the army out without going out
   himself, and he was idle, walking about on the roof, from where
   he could see Bathsheba bathing on a nearby roof.

4. Explain how David had the *means* to murder Uriah.

   David had the ability to send a message to Joab (by the hand
   of Uriah), with the authority to command Joab to abandon
   Uriah where the fighting was hardest, and the knowledge of
   how battles take place in order for his plan to succeed.

5. What pleasure(s) provided David's primary *motive* for these wrongs?

   He was motivated by sexual pleasure in the committing of
   adultery with Bathsheba, and he murdered Uriah in order to
   cover up this wrong.

6. What was David's state of mind when committing these wrongs?

   He thought he could do it without being found out by those
   who could do something about it (e.g., hiding the adultery
   by trying to get Uriah to sleep with his pregnant wife and
   hiding the murder by having the Ammonites kill Uriah for him),
   and he thought that, if found out, he could escape punishment
   because he was the king. David may have been encouraged

by his good reputation.

7. Why was David's murder of Uriah a *greater wrong* than a typical murder?

This murder involved David in special shame since Uriah was a loyal subject and one of David's mighty men (see 2 Samuel 23:39). It was also a compounded wrong of adultery plus murder. It was especially deliberate; David knew what he was doing.

8. To which primary *class of victim* did Bathsheba and Uriah each belong?

Bathsheba was pleasant to wrong, and she did not take precautions (bathing in sight of David). Uriah was easy to wrong; he trusted David, and after his death he could not prosecute.

9. David did not try to defend himself, but simply confessed and repented. What might a lesser man have said in defense of himself, appealing to *equity*?

David could have argued, "Be merciful to me. I was weak, tempted beyond what I could bear. I have never done any wickedness like this before. Think of all the good things that I have done for my people."

EXERCISE 14B

NAME

DATE

Read Cicero's First Oration against Catiline, and answer the following questions. Defend your answers.

1. Explain why Cicero's speech is an example of *forensic oratory* (consider the description of forensic oratory from the third paragraph of this lesson).

   <u>A forensic speech either accuses or defends someone based on the justice or injustice of his past actions. Cicero accuses Catiline, seeking to show the injustice of his past actions against himself and Rome. He does so before the Senate, which could judge the actions.</u>

2. Name three wrongs (or planned wrongs) for which Cicero accuses Catiline. Choose one, and explain how it fits the elements of the definition of *wrongdoing* (use the same wrong act for questions 3–5).

   <u>Cicero accuses Catiline of conspiracy, plotting the slaughter of the Senate, murdering Roman citizens, planning to kill Cicero, planning to destroy the city, and other wrongs. Killing Cicero is obviously an injury, it was voluntary (Catiline apparently tried to do it several times in different ways), and it is contrary to written and unwritten law.</u>

47

3. Explain how Catiline had or hoped to have the *means* to commit this wrong.

    Catiline had put himself at the head of a band of evil men with whom he conspired. He thought he had the ability to slay Cicero in his bed at the hand of two Roman knights. He also apparently tried to have Cicero stabbed.

4. What pleasure(s) provided Catiline's *motive* for committing these wrongs?

    Catiline may have wanted to get revenge on Cicero for gaining the consulship ahead of him. Catiline wanted power over others.

5. What was Catiline's primary *state of mind* when committing this wrong?

    Catiline apparently believed at first that he could carry out his plans without being found out, since he was trying to make these plans in secret. But after he was discovered, he probably thought that he could escape punishment, since he would have power.

6. To which *class of victim* did Cicero belong in regard to Catiline's attempted murder of him?

    Cicero would have been pleasant to wrong. It is pleasant to wrong those against whom we have grievances, and apparently Catiline had many grievances against Cicero.

_____

_____

7. Name three techniques that Cicero uses to argue that Catiline's acts were a *greater wrong*?

<u>Cicero makes Catiline's crimes appear worse by arguing that</u>
<u>they would cause great harm; Catiline, in the eyes of Rome,</u>
<u>was the only man to commit such crimes; it was not the</u>
<u>first time he had tried to commit such crimes; his acts were</u>
<u>especially deliberate; he was wronging his country; his crimes</u>
<u>were brazen, being committed in the Senate.</u>

_____

_____

8. Which of the *nontechnical means of persuasion* does Cicero employ in this speech?

<u>Cicero appeals to written law, the "resolution of the Senate,</u>
<u>a formidable and authoritative decree against you, O Catiline."</u>
<u>Cicero also clearly has information from witnesses, given the</u>
<u>details of what he knows of Catiline's conspiracy.</u>

_____

_____

EXERCISE 15A

NAME

DATE

Problems 1–2: Read through Christ's Sermon on the Mount, Matthew 5–7, and answer the following questions.

1. Appeal to the definition of political oratory to explain why this is a political speech. Defend your answer with biblical references.

   <u>Political oratory urges an assembly to do or not to do</u>
   <u>something based on expediency or harm. In the Sermon on</u>
   <u>the Mount, Jesus urges His disciples (Matthew 5:1–2) to walk in</u>
   <u>the ways of His Kingdom (6:33, 7:14) and the will of His Father</u>
   <u>(7:21) and not in faithless disobedience (5:21–32) so that God</u>
   <u>would be glorified, (5:16) and that He would provide them with</u>
   <u>good things (7:7–11).</u>

2. Identify ten distinct good things (not necessarily from Aristotle's list) promised in this speech to those who faithfully obey God. Include references.

   <u>(Answers may vary.)</u>
   1. <u>The kingdom of heaven (5:3)</u>
   2. <u>Comfort (5:4)</u>
   3. <u>The earth (5:5)</u>
   4. <u>Righteousness (5:6)</u>
   5. <u>God's mercy (5:7)</u>
   6. <u>Greatness in the kingdom (5:19)</u>

7. Being God's sons (5:45)
8. Open rewards (6:4, 6, 18)
9. Forgiveness (6:14)
10. Food and clothing (6:31–33)

Problems 3–4: Read Exodus 18:13–23, and answer the following questions.

3. What does Jethro, Moses' father-in-law, urge him not to do because of harm? What does he urge him to do out of expediency?

    Jethro urges Moses not to judge the people alone, lest he and they wear themselves out. Rather, he urges him to judge the hard cases and to assign God-fearing judges over smaller matters so that he can endure the work and satisfy the people.

4. To which *admittedly* good thing does Jethro appeal? To which *disputably* good thing? Defend your answers.

    Jethro says that if Moses does this, the people will receive the admitted good of justice (Exodus 18:22–23). Also, this way justice can be more easily done (18:22), a disputed good.

Problems 5–9: Read Deuteronomy 30:11–20, and answer the following questions.

5. Appeal to the definition of political oratory to explain why this is a political speech. Defend your answer with references.

> Political oratory urges an assembly to do or not to do
> something based on expediency or harm. Moses here urges
> the assembled people of Israel (Deut. 29:2) to keep God's
> commands that they would be blessed (30:16) and not to turn
> away to other gods and perish (30:17–18). Expediency or harm
> is presented in terms of blessing and cursing (30:19).

6. Which of Aristotle's *definitions of happiness* could one argue that Moses is appealing to? Explain.

> Moses appeals to good condition of property and body. Twice
> he promises that if the people obey God, He will give them
> long life, i.e., good condition of body; and blessing in the land,
> i.e., good condition of property (30:16, 20).

7. Which of Aristotle's *constituent parts of happiness* could one argue that Moses is appealing to? Defend your answer with references.

> One could argue that Moses is appealing to many children
> ("live and multiply"—30:16; "you and your descendants"—30:19)
> and to happy old age ("He is your life and the length of your
> days"—30:20)

8. Other than the constituent parts of happiness, which primary *admittedly good thing* does Moses appeal to? Defend your answer with references.

   More than anything else, Moses offers them "life itself" (30:16, 19–20).

9. Which *disputably good things* does Moses appeal to? Defend your answer with references.

   Moses appeals to the contrary of which is bad (i.e., "death and evil"—30:15); that which men deliberately choose to do (30:19); things that can be easily done (30:11–14).

EXERCISE 15B

NAME

DATE

Read "Give Me Liberty" by Patrick Henry, and answer the following questions. Defend your answers with appropriate quotations from the speech.

1. Which *definition of happiness* does Patrick Henry most appeal to?

    Henry appeals to independence of life when he argues, "If we wish to be free ..." and "as for me, give me liberty or give me death."

2. Identify two or three *constituent parts of happiness* that Henry argues his hearers will gain.

    He appeals to honor: "if we mean not basely to abandon the noble struggle in which we have been so long engaged, and which we have pledged ourselves never to abandon until the glorious object of our contest shall be obtained, we must fight!" He argues that God will give them strength: "Sir, we are not weak, if we make a proper use of the means which the God of nature hath placed in our power." He also says that God will give us good friends: "There is a just God ... who will raise up friends to fight our battles for us."

3. Which of the *definitions of goodness* does Henry appear to have in mind in this speech?

   <u>That for the sake of which we choose something else: "If we</u>
   <u>wish to be free ... we must fight!" Or, possibly, that which must</u>
   <u>be prescribed for a given individual by reason: "I know not</u>
   <u>what course others may take; but as for me, give me liberty,</u>
   <u>or give me death!"</u>

4. In his final paragraph, Patrick Henry argues that one good is greater than another. Name these *contrasting goods*, and identify one of Aristotle's greater goods that support Henry's position.

   <u>The contrasting goods are life and peace versus liberty.</u>
   <u>Aristotle says, "That is the greater good whose contrary is</u>
   <u>the greater evil, and whose loss affects us more." Henry argues</u>
   <u>that the contrary of liberty—"chains and slavery"—is a</u>
   <u>greater evil than the contrary of life: "Give me liberty, or give</u>
   <u>me death!"</u>

EXERCISE 16A

NAME

DATE

Read this excerpt in praise of Isaac Newton from Petr Beckmann's *A History of Pi*, chapter 13, and answer the questions. Defend each of your answers using quotes from the excerpt.

There had never been a scientist like Newton, and there has not been one like him since. Not Einstein, not Archimedes, not Galileo, not Planck, not anybody else measured up to anywhere near his stature. Indeed, it is safe to say that there can never be a scientist like Newton again, for the scientists of future generations will have books and libraries, microfilms and microfiches, magnetic discs and other computerized information to draw on. Newton had nothing, nothing except Galileo's qualitative thoughts and Kepler's laws of planetary motion. With little more than that to go on, Newton formulated three laws that govern all motion in the universe: From the galaxies in the heavens to the electrons whirling round atomic nuclei, from the cat that always falls on its feet to the gyroscopes that watch over the flight of space ships. His laws of motion have withstood the test of time for three centuries. The very concepts of space, time and mass have crumbled under the impact of Einstein's theory of relativity; age-old prejudices of cause, effect and certainty were destroyed by quantum mechanics; but Newton's laws have come through unscathed....

Newton's achievement in discovering the differential and integral calculus is, in comparison, a smaller achievement; even so, it was epochal. As we have seen, the ground was well prepared for its discovery by a sizable troop of pioneers. Leibniz discovered it independently of Newton some ten years later, and Newton would not have been the giant he was if he had overlooked it. For Newton overlooked nothing. He found all the big things that were to be found in his time, and a host of lesser things (such as a way to calculate pi) as well. How many more his ever-brooding mind discovered, we shall never know, for he had an almost obsessive aversion to publishing his works. The greatest scientific book ever published, his Principia, took definite shape in his mind in 1665, when he was 23; but he did not commit his theories to paper until 1672–74. Whether he wrote them down for his own satisfaction or for posterity, we do not know, but the manuscript (of Part 1) lay in his drawer for ten more years, until his friend Edmond Halley

(1656–1742) accidentally learned of its existence in 1684. Halley was one of the world's great astronomers; yet his greatest contribution to science was persuading Newton to publish the Principia, urging him to finish the second and third parts, seeing them through the press, and financing their publication. In 1687 this greatest of all scientific works came off the press and heralded the birth of modern science.

Isaac Newton was born on Christmas Day, 1642, in a small farm house at Woolsthorpe near Colsterworth, Lincolnshire. At Grantham, the nearest place that had a school, he did not excel in mathematics in the dazzling way of the wonderchildren Pascal or Gauss, but his schoolmaster, Mr. Stokes, noticed that the boy was bright. If there was any omen of young Isaac's future destiny, it must have been his habit of brooding. Going home from Grantham, it was usual to dismount and lead one's horse up a particularly steep hill. But Isaac would occasionally be so deeply lost in meditation that he would forget to remount his horse and walk home the rest of the way.

When he finished school, there came the great turning point of Newton's career. His widowed mother wanted him to take over the farm, but Stokes was able to persuade her to send Isaac to Cambridge, where he was very quickly through with Euclid, and soon he mastered Descartes' new geometry. By the time he was twenty-one, he had discovered the binomial theorem for fractional powers, and had embarked on his discovery of infinite series and "fluxions" (derivatives). Soon he was correcting, and adding to, the work of his professor and friend, Isaac Barrow. In 1665 the Great Plague broke out, in Cambridge as well as London, and the university was closed down. Newton returned to Woolsthorpe for the rest of the year and part of the next. It is most probable that during this time, when he was twenty-three, with no one about but his mother to disturb his brooding, Newton made the greater part of his vast discoveries. "All this was in the two plague years 1665 and 1666," he reminisced in old age, "for in those days I was in the prime of my age of invention, and minded mathematics and [natural] philosophy more than at any time since." Asked how he made his discoveries, he answered, "By always thinking unto them," and on another occasion, "I keep the subject constantly before me and wait till the first dawnings open little by little into the full light." Newton retained these great powers of concentration through-out his life. He succeeded Barrow as Lucasian Professor of Mathematics at Cambridge (1669), and relinquished this post to become Warden of the Mint (1696) and later (1699) Master of the Mint; in 1703 he was elected President of the Royal Society, a position which he held until his death in 1726. In his later years he spent much time on non-scientific activity, but remained as astute a mathematician as ever, amazing men by the ease with which he solved problems set up to challenge him.

In 1697, for example, Jean Bernoulli I (1667–1748) posed a problem that was to become famous in the founding of the Calculus of Variations: What is the curve joining two given points such that a heavy particle will move along the curve from the upper to the lower point in minimum time? The problem is so difficult that it is not, for example, usually included in to-day's under-graduate engineering curriculum. It was received by the Royal Society and handed to Newton in the afternoon; he returned the solution the next morning, and according to John Conduitt (his niece's husband), he solved it before going to bed! The solution was sent to Jean Bernoulli without signature, but on reading it he instantly recognized the author, as he exclaimed, *tanquam ex ungue leonem* (as the lion is known by its claw).

1. Which of Aristotle's forms of virtue does Beckmann primarily employ in praise of Newton?

   Wisdom, especially scientific wisdom. "Newton formulated three laws that govern all motion in the universe" etc. (An argument could be made for temperance.)

2. Beckmann praises Newton using many of the noble deeds identified by Aristotle. Identify eight of them.

   1) Things that deserve to be remembered—"His laws of motion have stood the test of time for three centuries."
   2) Things that are exceptional—Many other scientific theories have been disproven, "but Newton's laws have come through unscathed."
   3) Successes which benefit others—"In 1687 this greatest of all scientific works came off the press and heralded the birth of modern science."
   4) Actions appropriate to the man who does them—"Newton

would not have been the giant he was if he had overlooked it.
For Newton overlooked nothing."

5) Qualities which give more pleasure to others than to their
possessors—"...for he had an almost obsessive aversion to
publishing his works"

6) Services done for one's benefactors—"Soon he was
correcting, and adding to, the work of his professor and
friend, Isaac Barrow."

7) Actions worthy of his own past career—"In his later
years he ...remained as astute a mathematician as ever,
amazing men by the ease with which he solved problems."

8) Victory—"He returned the solution the next morning."

_____

_____

_____

_____

_____

_____

_____

_____

_____

Problems 3–8: Beckmann also uses many methods to improve on his praise of
Newton by pointing out how he was unique. Quote from the excerpt where he
uses each given method.

3. He is the first one

   "Newton's achievement in discovering the differential and
   integral calculus is, in comparison, a smaller achievement; even

so, it was epochal.

4. He is the only one

   "There had never been a scientist like Newton, and there has not been one like him since."

5. He has done it better than anyone else

   "The greatest scientific work every published, his Principia ..."

6. He has succeeded in this same way often

   "He found all the big things that were to be found in his time, and a host of lesser things as well."

7. Unexpected success given the circumstances

   "Newton had nothing, nothing except Galileo's qualitative thoughts and Kepler's laws of planetary motion. With little more than that to go on, Newton formulated three laws ..."

8. Compare him with great men

   "Not Einstein, not Archimedes, not Galileo, not Planck, not anybody else measured up to anywhere near his stature."

EXERCISE 16B

NAME

DATE

Read this speech in praise of Gerhard Groote by Dr. George Grant[1] and answer the questions. Defend each of your answers using quotes from the speech.

Some men's greatness may be seen in how largely they loom over the movements they launched. But greater men are they whose movements loom large over them—even to the point of obscuring them from view.

Gerhard Groote was just such a man. It would be difficult to find a single page of modern history written about him. But it would be even more difficult to find a single page of modern history that has not been profoundly affected by him. He lived in the tumultuous days of the fourteenth century. A contemporary of John Wycliffe, Geoffrey Chaucer, and Jan Hus, he saw the scourge of the Black Death sweep a quarter of the population of the world away in a wave of pestilence; he saw France and England locked in the intractable conflagration of the Hundred Years War; he saw the Western church sundered by the Great Schism that produced two, sometimes three, sometimes even four, popes; and he saw the rise of the universities and the smothering influence of humanistic scholasticism. Churches were riven by corruption, kingdoms were shaken by instability, families were splintered by adversity, and the very foundations of Christian civilization in the West seemed to be crumbling.

They were dire days indeed. The problems facing men and nations seemed all but insurmountable. Doomsayers had a heyday. Sound familiar?

Groote was raised in the home of a prosperous merchant and received the finest education available. Alas, he found it difficult to take the claims of his academic masters, his ecclesiastical mentors, and his church peers seriously. Like so many of his contemporaries, he concluded that the overt wickedness of the church and the blatant debauchery of the university mitigated against any serious belief in the gospel. As a result, he ran from conviction and spent his youth and his wealth on reckless and heedless dissipation. He moved progressively from spoiled brat to party animal to insufferable boor. When he was finally arrested by grace and converted, he had tasted all the pleasures the medieval world had to offer—and still he yearned for more.

1 From Ligonier Ministries and R.C. Sproul. © *Tabletalk* magazine. Website: www.ligonier.org /tabletalk. Email: tabletalk@ligonier.org. Toll free: 1-800-435-4343. Used with permission.

As an ardent new convert in the midst of a church awash in promiscuous impiety, he lifted up an urgent prophetic voice against the evils of his day. He began to model a life of radical discipleship. And he attracted a strong following in his native Dutch lowlands.

Eventually, Groote's movement came to be known as the Brethren of the Common Life. He and his followers were committed to the authority of the Scriptures first and foremost. They promoted biblical preaching that was practical and accessible to the ordinary Christian. They pioneered vernacular translations of the Bible. And they founded schools to educate young men and women to be wise and discerning believers as well as effective and successful citizens.

The revival wrought by the movement was genuine, vibrant, and even widely admired. Even so, it could hardly have been expected to put a dent in the overwhelming problems of the day. Indeed, the litany of fourteenth century woes continued, seemingly unabated. When Groote died, some asserted that his efforts at renewal were ultimately stymied by the fierce reality of the circumstances of the day; he was by all such accounts, a failure.

But throughout his life and ministry, Groote was laying foundations for something that might endure well beyond his own life and ministry. He had a multigenerational plan. He understood that it had taken a very long time for Western civilization to get into the mess that it was in and that no man or movement, no matter how potent or effective, would be able to turn things around overnight. That was why the heart and soul of his plan was to disseminate the Scriptures and build schools. His covenantal theology had led him to have a generational vision, one that enabled him to invest in a future he would likely never see on this earth.

It was a wise strategy. Amazingly, in less than a century and a half the strategy began to bear abundant fruit: it was in those scattered and seemingly insignificant Brethren of Common Life schools that nearly every one of the magisterial reformers would ultimately be educated: Luther, Zwingli, Calvin, Melancthon, Bucer, and Beza.

An obscure man changed the course of history—albeit generations later—by simply living out the implications of radical grace and covenantal faithfulness right where he was. He faced the impossible odds of a culture gone terribly awry. He implemented a generational vision that laid new foundations for freedom and prosperity simply by equipping and enabling future leaders.

Perhaps by looking back at Groote and his reforming work, we will be able to see our way forward for our own. After all, his was a distinctly biblical vision, a sound vision, and thus a rather unpopular vision. And it still is.

1. Identify two of Aristotle's forms of virtue that Grant employs in praise of Groote.

    Wisdom—"It was a wise strategy."

    Prudence—"But throughout his life and ministry, Groote
    was laying foundations for something that might endure well
    beyond his own life and ministry."

2. Identify eight of the noble deeds identified by Aristotle that Grant uses in praise of Groote.

    1) Things that continue after death—"But it would be even
    more difficult to find a single page of modern history that has
    not been profoundly affected by him."

    2) Actions worthy of his ancestors—"Groote was raised in
    the home of a prosperous merchant and received the finest
    education available."

    3) The opposites of those things of which men feel
    ashamed—"As an ardent new convert in the midst of a church
    awash in promiscuous impiety..."

    4) Aiming at something desirable for someone else's sake—
    "He began to model a life of radical discipleship."

    5) Actions done for the sake of others—"They promoted
    biblical preaching that was practical and accessible to the
    ordinary Christian."

    6) Successes which benefit others—"It was in those ...
    Brethren of Common Life schools that nearly every one of the
    magisterial reformers would ultimately be educated."

    7) Honor—"The revival wrought by the movement was
    genuine, vibrant, and even widely admired."

8) Things that are exceptional—"After all, his was a distinctly biblical vision, a sound vision, and thus a rather unpopular vision. And it still is."

Problems 3–6: Grant also uses many methods to improve on his praise of Groote by pointing out how he was unique. Quote from the excerpt where he uses each given method.

3. He is the first one

   "They pioneered vernacular translations of the Bible."

4. He has done it better than anyone else

   "But greater men are they whose movements loom large over them—even to the point of obscuring them from view. Gerhard Groote was just such a man."

5. He has succeeded in this same way often

    "In the Brethren of Common Life schools nearly every one of the magisterial reformers would ultimately be educated: Luther, Zwingli, Calvin, Melancthon, Bucer, and Beza."

6. Unexpected success given the circumstances

    "Even so, it could hardly have been expected to put a dent in the overwhelming problems of the day. Indeed, the litany of fourteenth century woes continued, seemingly unabated."

7. In a couple of places Grant connects his praise of Groote with modern times, creating in his audience a spirit of emulation. Does this improve the effectiveness of his praise? Compare this method with Beckmann's approach to praising Isaac Newton.

    Producing in his audience feelings of emulation does seem to improve the effectiveness of his praise. Unlike the speech in praise of Newton, whom Beckmann lifted up higher than any other scientist, Grant presents Groote as a man who lived in times much like our own, whose success depended not on being a mathematical genius but simply on living a life of "radical discipleship" following a sinful, misspent youth—a life not unlike many of us today. We also are able to believe the authority of Scripture, promote biblical reading, and found schools. Grant's closing really drives the point home: Groote's vision was biblical, sound, and unpopular, and it still is. We may have a similar experience, with similar struggles. But if

we trust God like Groote did, the Lord may see fit to bless
our labor in similar ways. This makes Groote more like a hero
worthy of imitation, rather than an unreachably high giant.

EXERCISE 17A

NAME

DATE

Problems 1–3: For each of the given terms, identify at least three *parts* (or elements or steps) in the left column, and at least three *species* in the right column. Be careful to use consistent dividing principles.

1. Speech

Speaker	Political speech
Audience	Forensic speech
Message	Ceremonial speech

2. Sound

Loudness	Discordant sound
Pitch	Instrumental music
Quality	Vocal music

3. Dinner

Appetizer	Home dinner
Main dish	Picnic dinner
Dessert	Restaurant dinner

4. Define *monarchy* in the following ways:

Example United Kingdom, Jordan, Israel (under Solomon)

Etymology mon (one) + archy (rule) = rule by one

Genus and difference Form of government in which one person rules, such as a king or queen

69

Problems 5–6: Read through Patrick Henry's "Give Me Liberty" speech (see Appendix A of the text), then answer the questions, quoting the appropriate passage from the speech.

5. What term does Henry define (or clarify) with repeated synonyms? List the synonyms.

    The word "petition." The synonyms (or near synonyms) are
    remonstration, supplication, prostration, imploring.

6. Henry defined "to be free" with a genus and difference definition. What other term does he clarify by providing a genus and difference definition? What is his definition?

    The term "weak," which he defines as "unable to cope with an
    adversary."

EXERCISE 17B

NAME

DATE

Read this excerpt from Martin Luther King Jr.'s Letter from Birmingham Jail, and answer the questions.

> I think I should indicate why I am here in Birmingham, since you have been influenced by the view which argues against "outsiders coming in."... Several months ago the affiliate here in Birmingham asked us to be on call to engage in a nonviolent direct action program if such were deemed necessary. We readily consented, and when the hour came we lived up to our promise. So I, along with several members of my staff, am here because I was invited here. I am here because I have organizational ties here.
>
> But more basically, I am in Birmingham because injustice is here. Just as the prophets of the eighth century B.C. left their villages and carried their "thus saith the Lord" far beyond the boundaries of their home towns, and just as the Apostle Paul left his village of Tarsus and carried the gospel of Jesus Christ to the far corners of the Greco Roman world, so am I compelled to carry the gospel of freedom beyond my own home town. Like Paul, I must constantly respond to the Macedonian call for aid.
>
> Moreover, I am cognizant of the interrelatedness of all communities and states. I cannot sit idly by in Atlanta and not be concerned about what happens in Birmingham. Injustice anywhere is a threat to justice everywhere. We are caught in an inescapable network of mutuality, tied in a single garment of destiny. Whatever affects one directly, affects all indirectly. Never again can we afford to live with the narrow, provincial "outside agitator" idea. Anyone who lives inside the United States can never be considered an outsider anywhere within its bounds....

1. The word "outsider" is vague. How would the opponents of Dr. King define this term? How does he redefine this term? Explain how his redefinition helps to make his rhetorical point.

   <u>His opponents may have defined outsider as "a person who is</u>
   <u>not a member of the local community." Dr. King redefines the</u>
   <u>term as "a person who has no interest in the good of the</u>

community," especially one who lives outside the United States. He uses this idea to effectively argue that he has such an interest because he was invited to help, has organizational ties, and is compelled to help by the perceived need as an American. Thus, he is not really an outsider.

_____

_____

_____

_____

_____

Now do the same for this excerpt.

In any nonviolent campaign there are four basic steps: collection of the facts to determine whether injustices exist; negotiation; self-purification; and direct action. We have gone through all these steps in Birmingham. There can be no gainsaying the fact that racial injustice engulfs this community. Birmingham is probably the most thoroughly segregated city in the United States. Its ugly record of brutality is widely known. Negroes have experienced grossly unjust treatment in the courts. There have been more unsolved bombings of Negro homes and churches in Birmingham than in any other city in the nation. These are the hard, brutal facts of the case. On the basis of these conditions, Negro leaders sought to negotiate with the city fathers. But the latter consistently refused to engage in good faith negotiation....

Mindful of the difficulties involved, we decided to undertake a process of self-purification. We began a series of workshops on nonviolence, and we repeatedly asked ourselves: "Are you able to accept blows without retaliating?" "Are you able to endure the ordeal of jail?" We decided to schedule our direct action program for the Easter season, realizing that except for Christmas, this is the main shopping period of the year. Knowing that a strong economic-withdrawal program would be the by-product of direct action, we felt that this would be the best time to bring pressure to bear on the merchants for the needed change....

2. Dr. King identifies four steps of a nonviolent campaign. Explain how each step leads to the next.

The four steps are collection of facts, negotiation, self-purification, and direct action. The collection of facts leads to the discovery of any injustices in the community. If they find significant injustice, they seek to negotiate with community leaders to remove the causes of the injustice. If negotiation fails, they undertake a process of self-purification. After they are prepared, they commit to direct action to bring pressure for change.

Read this final excerpt, and answer the questions.

You express a great deal of anxiety over our willingness to break laws. This is certainly a legitimate concern. Since we so diligently urge people to obey the Supreme Court's decision of 1954 outlawing segregation in the public schools, at first glance it may seem rather paradoxical for us consciously to break laws. One may well ask: "How can you advocate breaking some laws and obeying others?" The answer lies in the fact that there are two types of laws: just and unjust. I would be the first to advocate obeying just laws. One has not only a legal but a moral responsibility to obey just laws. Conversely, one has a moral responsibility to disobey unjust laws. I would agree with St. Augustine that "an unjust law is no law at all."

Now, what is the difference between the two? How does one determine whether a law is just or unjust? A just law is a man-made code that squares with the moral law or the law of God. An unjust law is a code that is out of harmony with the moral law. To put it in the terms of St. Thomas Aquinas: An unjust law is a human law that is not rooted in eternal law and natural law. Any law that uplifts human personality is just. Any law that degrades human personality is unjust...Thus it is that I can urge men to obey the

1954 decision of the Supreme Court, for it is morally right; and I can urge them to disobey segregation ordinances, for they are morally wrong....

Of course, there is nothing new about this kind of civil disobedience. It was evidenced sublimely in the refusal of Shadrach, Meshach and Abednego to obey the laws of Nebuchadnezzar, on the ground that a higher moral law was at stake. It was practiced superbly by the early Christians, who were willing to face hungry lions and the excruciating pain of chopping blocks rather than submit to certain unjust laws of the Roman Empire. To a degree, academic freedom is a reality today because Socrates practiced civil disobedience. In our own nation, the Boston Tea Party represented a massive act of civil disobedience...

3. What are the two species of law that Dr. King identifies? Identify three dividing principles he uses to distinguish them.

    The two species of law are just and unjust. Three of his

    dividing principles are:

    1. Whether it is in harmony with God's moral law or not

    2. Whether it is rooted in eternal law (or natural law) or not

    3. Whether it uplifts human personality or degrades it

EXERCISE 18A

NAME

DATE

Problems 1–8: Identify the statements as *simple* or *compound* by circling the correct choice.

1. We are met on a great battlefield of that war.

    (simple)   compound

2. The world will little note, nor long remember, what we say here.

    simple   (compound)

3. There is a just God who presides over the destinies of nations.

    (simple)   compound

4. An appeal to arms and to the God of hosts is all that is left us!

    simple   (compound)

5. I will prove it if you do deny it.

    simple   (compound)

6. The consul orders an enemy to depart from the city.

    (simple)   compound

7. Injustice anywhere is a threat to justice everywhere.

    (simple)   compound

8. Time can be used either destructively or constructively.

    simple   (compound)

Problems 9–13: Write whether the statements from the Bible are *singular* or *indefinite*. If they are indefinite, write whether the statement should be considered *particular* or *universal*.

9. The rulers take counsel together against the Lord and against His Anointed. (Psalm 2:2)

    indefinite, particular

10. Righteousness exalts a nation. (Proverbs 14:34)

    indefinite, universal

11. Babylon has caused the slain of Israel to fall. (Jeremiah 51:49)

    singular

12. The lamp of the body is the eye. (Matthew 6:22)

    singular

13. The dead were judged according to their works. (Revelation 20:12)

    indefinite, universal

EXERCISE 18B

1. Read Acts 26:25–32 below. Identify each **bold** compound statement as a *conjunction, disjunction,* or *conditional.*

²⁵ "I am not insane, most excellent Festus," Paul replied. "**What I am saying is true and reasonable.** ²⁶ The king is familiar with these things, and I can speak freely to him. I am convinced that none of this has escaped his notice, because it was not done in a corner. ²⁷ King Agrippa, do you believe the prophets? I know you do."

²⁸ Then Agrippa said to Paul, "Do you think that in such a short time you can persuade me to be a Christian?"

²⁹ Paul replied, "Short time or long— **I pray to God that not only you but all who are listening to me today may become what I am,** except for these chains."

³⁰ The king rose, and with him the governor and Bernice and those sitting with them. ³¹ After they left the room, they began saying to one another, "**This man is not doing anything that deserves death or imprisonment.**"

³² Agrippa said to Festus, "**This man could have been set free if he had not appealed to Caesar.**"

conjunction _____

conjunction _____

disjunction _____

conditional _____

Problems 2–3: Combine the two statements by rewriting them into a single *biconditional*. (Ignore minor additional details and different wording. Write in normal sounding language.)

2. "If you surely surrender to the king of Babylon's princes, then your soul shall live; this city shall not be burned with fire, and you and your house shall live. But if you do not surrender to the king of Babylon's princes, then this city shall be given into the hand of the Chaldeans; they shall burn it with fire, and you shall not escape from their hand" (Jeremiah 38:17–18).

    <u>This city shall not be burned with fire, and you shall live if and only if you surrender to the king of Babylon's princes.</u>

3. "For if you forgive men their trespasses, your heavenly Father will also forgive you. But if you do not forgive men their trespasses, neither will your Father forgive your trespasses" (Matthew 6:14–15).

    <u>Your heavenly Father will forgive your trespasses if and only if you forgive men their trespasses.</u>

Problems 4–12: Identify the most specific relationship between the given pair of statements from this list: *contradiction, contrariety, equivalence, implication, independence, subcontrariety.*

4. All mechanical things break. / Some mechanical things do not break.

    <u>contradiction</u>

5. Some mathematicians are engineers. / Some engineers are mathematicians.

    <u>equivalence</u>

6. Everybody loves a winner. / Nobody loves a winner.

    <u>contrariety</u>

7. Sometimes you just can't win. / Sometimes you can win.

   subcontrariety

8. This man Zechariah has a son. / This man Zechariah is a father.

   implication

9. Jane is a wife. / Jane has a sister-in-law.

   independence

10. Some desperados are renegades. / No desperados are renegades.

    contradiction

11. Martin is neither a priest nor a soldier. / Martin is not a soldier.

    implication

12. He is a good director if and only if he is an experienced actor. / He is an experienced actor.

    independence

13. Identify by problem number (4–12) which of the above pair of statements are consistent. 5, 7, 8, 9, 11, 12

EXERCISE 19A

NAME

DATE

For each given statement from the Declaration of Independence, identify the method by which the author Thomas Jefferson came to know the truth of it. Be specific. You may add a brief explanation for your answer. Also, you may be assisted by reading the statements in context.

1. "All men are created equal."

    Jefferson claimed that this was a self-evident truth. "We hold these truths to be self-evident ..."

2. "Governments long established should not be changed for light and transient causes."

    Inductive reasoning. Jefferson says this is dictated by prudence, but appeals to experience to support this truth in the next sentence.

3. "The history of the present king of Great Britain is a history of repeated injuries and usurpations, all having in direct object the establishment of an absolute tyranny over these States."

    Inductive reasoning. He proves this by listing facts based on the experience of the colonies' dealings with the king.

4. "He has kept among us, in times of peace, standing armies."

    Evidence of the senses. Jefferson no doubt saw such standing armies with his own eyes.

5. "He has constrained our fellow citizens taken captive on the high seas to bear arms against their country."

   Faith in authority. Jefferson himself probably never saw the
   impressment of Americans into the British navy, but likely
   learned about it from others.

6. "These United Colonies are, and of right ought to be free and independent states."

   Deductive reasoning. This follows from the argument of the
   entire Declaration of Independence.

EXERCISE 19B

NAME

DATE

Problems 1–4: Argue for the truth of the given statement by appealing to an equivalent statement, identified as *converse, obverse,* or *contrapositive* (use each at least once). Use ordinary language. (Answers may vary.)

1. All His ways are justice. (Deuteronomy 32:4)

   <u>All His ways are justice for all injustice is against the ways of</u>
   <u>God. Contrapositive.</u>

2. No one who puts his hand to the plow and looks back is fit for the kingdom of God. (Luke 9:62)

   <u>No one who puts his hand to the plow and looks back is fit</u>
   <u>for the kingdom of God since all who look back after putting</u>
   <u>their hand to the plow are unfit for God's kingdom. Obverse.</u>

3. Some of the king's servants are dead. (2 Samuel 11:24)

   <u>Some of the king's servants are dead because some found</u>
   <u>among the dead were the king's servants. Converse.</u>

4. Some disciples do not believe. (John 6:64)

   <u>Some disciples do not believe because some unbelievers were</u>
   <u>not absent from the disciples. Contrapositive.</u>

83

Problems 5–10: For the given statement, write a different but equivalent statement.

5. You shall not kill both the cow and her young on the same day. (Leviticus 22:28)

   On the same day you shall either not kill the cow or you shall not kill her young.

6. You have neither heard His voice at any time, nor seen His form. (John 5:37)

   You did not hear His voice at any time, and you did not see His form.

7. If that first covenant had been faultless, then no place would have been sought for a second. (Hebrews 8:7)

   If a place was sought for a second covenant, then the first covenant was faulty.

8. The law is good if one uses it lawfully. (1 Timothy 1:8)

   If one uses it lawfully, then the law is good.

9. Unless one is born again, he cannot see the kingdom of God. (John 3:3)

   If one can see the kingdom of God, then one has been born again.

10. If, while her husband lives, she marries another man, she is an adulteress; but if her husband dies, she is no adulteress, though she has married another man. (Romans 7:3)

    A woman is an adulteress if and only if she marries another man while her husband lives.

Problems 11–14: Use the given general line of argument to argue for the given statement. Write the argument in if–then form, with the given statement as the consequent. (Answers may vary)

11. He who does good unwittingly does not deserve a reward. (Opposites)

    If he who does harm unwittingly does not deserve to be punished, then he who does good unwittingly does not deserve a reward.

12. The church is free to use the congregation's tithes as they see fit. (Correlative ideas)

    If the congregation gives tithes freely and without restriction, then the church is free to use those tithes as they see fit.

13. Schools must allow boys to join the volleyball team. (Rational correspondence)

    If schools allow girls to join the football team, then they must allow boys to join the volleyball team.

14. It is wrong to slander your friends. (*A fortiori*)

<u>If it is wrong to slander your enemies, how much more is it</u>
<u>wrong to slander your friends!</u>

EXERCISE 20

NAME

DATE

Problems 1–4: For each type of maxim, give an example along with a brief explanation of why the maxim is of that type. You may find your own or select them from the list of 100 maxims. (Answers may vary.)

1. Known truth _"Easier said than done" is a well-known, generally agreed upon saying. Most people have known someone who talked about big plans, only to find that executing those plans was more difficult than they anticipated._

2. Clear at a glance _"The apple doesn't fall far from the tree." This is one of the lesser known maxims, but it is obviously true in its literal sense, and it makes immediate metaphorical sense that a child will imitate his parent._

3. Paradoxical _"Actions speak louder than words" is literally self-contradictory, since we only speak by means of words. But metaphorically it is true that what we do can tell more about our character than what we say._

4. Disputable <u>"Birds of a feather flock together." While it is</u>
<u>sometimes true that people enjoying being in the company</u>
<u>of others like them, it is also sometimes true that "opposites</u>
<u>attract."</u>

5. Give an example, different from the above, of two maxims from the list of 100 that appear to contradict. Explain how the maxims can be reconciled by a proper understanding of the context.

<u>"Absence makes the heart grow fonder" appears to disagree</u>
<u>with "Out of sight, out of mind." The first maxim is often true</u>
<u>when the absent friend is one we already have a strong bond</u>
<u>with so that we think about them when they are away. The</u>
<u>second can be true when a friendship is not as close, and</u>
<u>when we get busy making new friends who replace those who</u>
<u>are absent.</u>

6. Give examples of biblical maxims, one from the Old Testament and one from the New, which would be familiar to people who have not read the Bible. Include the references.

<u>"There is nothing new under the sun" (Eccles. 1:9).</u>
<u>"The spirit is willing, but the flesh is weak" (Matt. 26:41).</u>

7. Develop an enthymeme (an argument of one premise and one conclusion) by taking a maxim from the list of 100 and adding a brief explanation.

   <u>Good fences make good neighbors, because we feel more</u>
   <u>comfortable around those who will respect our privacy.</u>

   _____

   _____

8. Rewrite a maxim by removing some words. The new maxim must still make sense.

   <u>A penny saved is a penny.</u>

   _____

9. Refute a disputable maxim from the list of 100, adding an explanation of why it is wrong in the case supposed.

   <u>It is said that a rising tide lifts all boats, but this is not true</u>
   <u>if some of the boats have a hole in them. Improvements in</u>
   <u>the general economy may benefit those businesses that are</u>
   <u>already secure, but it may simply flood those businesses that</u>
   <u>are already struggling.</u>

   _____

   _____

   _____

EXERCISE 21A

NAME

DATE

Problems 1–3: Read this excerpt, an argument from actual past fact, from Martin Luther's *Here I Stand*, and answer the given questions.

> Let us have a care lest the reign of the young and noble prince, the emperor Charles, on whom, next to God, we build so many hopes, should not only commence, but continue and terminate its course under the most fatal auspices. I might cite examples drawn from the oracles of God. I might speak of pharaohs, of kings of Babylon, or of Israel, who were never more contributing to their own ruin that when, by measures in appearances most prudent, they thought to establish their authority!

1. Explain how the examples cited are relevantly similar to the point Luther is making.

   <u>In the examples given, the kings were trying to establish</u>
   <u>their own authority, but found themselves opposing God, which</u>
   <u>led to their ruin. Luther is warning the emperor against</u>
   <u>making the same mistake. He doesn't want Charles to try to</u>
   <u>establish his authority by opposing Luther and his writings</u>
   <u>against the Catholic Church.</u>

2. Locate a scriptural reference where each king from Luther's examples contributed to his ruin by seeking to establish his authority.

   Pharaoh of Egypt <u>Exodus 14</u>

   King of Babylon <u>Daniel 4:19–33</u>

   King of Israel <u>Kings 21:17–24</u>

3. By means of these examples, Luther subtly sides with the biblical heroes who opposed each of these kings. Identify the man he is likely identifying with who opposed each given king.

    Pharaoh of Egypt <u>Moses</u>

    King of Babylon <u>Daniel</u>

    King of Israel <u>Elijah</u>

Problems 4–5: Read this excerpt from Jonathan Edwards's sermon "Sinners in the Hand of an Angry God," and answer the given questions. (Line numbers are added for convenience.)

> [1]It is no security to wicked men for one moment, that there are no visible means of death at hand. [2]It is no security to a natural man, that he is now in health, and that he does not see which way he should now immediately go out of the world by any accident, and that there is no visible danger in any respect in his circumstances. [3]The manifold and continual experience of the world in all ages, shows this is no evidence, that a man is not on the very brink of eternity, and that the next step will not be into another world. [4]The unseen, unthought-of ways and means of persons going suddenly out of the world are innumerable and inconceivable. [5]Unconverted men walk over the pit of hell on a rotten covering, and there are innumerable places in this covering so weak that they will not bear their weight, and these places are not seen. [6]The arrows of death fly unseen at noon-day; the sharpest sight cannot discern them. [7]God has so many different unsearchable ways of taking wicked men out of the world and sending them to hell, that there is nothing to make it appear, that God had need to be at the expense of a miracle, or go out of the ordinary course of his providence, to destroy any wicked man, at any moment.

This excerpt contains two illustrative parallels. For each one identified, write out the source example and target conclusion behind the illustrative parallel.

4. From line 5

    Source <u>Unconverted men walk over the pit of hell on a rotten covering, and there are innumerable places in this covering so weak that they will not bear their weight, and these places</u>

are not seen.

Target <u>Unconverted men live their lives trusting in their health and other contrivances to keep them alive and out of hell. But they do not realize that their health or other contrivances could fail so that they could die and go there quickly.</u>

5. From line 6

    Source <u>The arrows of death fly unseen at noon-day; the sharpest sight cannot discern them.</u>

    Target <u>There are many means of death that people are unaware of, even though it seems like they can perceive them all clearly.</u>

EXERCISE 21B

NAME

DATE

Problems 1–4: For the three types of argument by example, come up with a single thesis statement that could be supported by them. Then write out each of the three types of argument. You may again use your thesis statement from Exercise 5 if it has the quality of a maxim. (Sample Answers)

1. Thesis <u>Always back up your computer work. One small mistake</u> <u>and you could lose it all.</u>

2. Mention of actual past fact <u>We all know people who have lost</u> <u>computer work because they did not save it before it was</u> <u>accidentally deleted. My friend lost an unsaved computer</u> <u>program when the teacher turned off the computer after my</u> <u>friend briefly left the room.</u>

3. Illustrative parallel <u>Not backing up your computer work is like</u> <u>leaving your money or valuables out in the open instead of</u> <u>putting them in a safe; what you value can all be easily stolen</u> <u>or lost accidentally.</u>

4. **Fable** <u>One late fall in the forest, a squirrel was running back</u>
<u>and forth on the tree branches, storing up his nuts in the</u>
<u>hollow of an old oak near his home. He was careful to keep</u>
<u>his storage place secret so that the nuts would not be stolen,</u>
<u>and to make the place deep and high in the strong tree. As</u>
<u>he was busy storing the product of his labors, he ran across</u>
<u>a rabbit returning from one of his visits to a nearby farmer's</u>
<u>garden. The rabbit had lots of carrots that he kept in some tall</u>
<u>grass outside his rabbit hole. The squirrel saw this and called</u>
<u>down to the rabbit, "Friend, shouldn't you put that produce in a</u>
<u>safe place? Anyone or anything could take them from you, and</u>
<u>all your labor will be in vain!" The rabbit replied, "Thank you</u>
<u>for your advice, but I have been keeping my carrots in this</u>
<u>grass for a long time, and nothing has ever happened to them."</u>
<u>But the very next day, when the rabbit was once again gone</u>
<u>to the garden, a rat came scuttling by, saw all the delicious</u>
<u>carrots, and carried off as many as he could to his home in the</u>
<u>farmer's shed. When the rabbit returned and saw the carrots</u>
<u>gone from the grassy place, he ran all over in a panic trying</u>
<u>to find where they all went, but to no avail. The squirrel came</u>
<u>to him and said, "Friend, if you had listened to me and taken a</u>
<u>little extra effort to keep the product of your work in a safe</u>
<u>place, you would not be enduring this sad loss." So you also</u>
<u>should keep your work safe and sound, for you never know</u>
<u>what might happen to it tomorrow.</u>

EXERCISE 22A

NAME

DATE

Problems 1–8: Underline the conclusion in the given categorical syllogism. These syllogisms will also be used for problems 9–16.

1. Given that all postmillennialists are preterists, and some postmillennialists are Presbyterians, it follows that <u>some Presbyterians are preterists.</u>

2. <u>Some loving fathers are not stay-at-home dads,</u> because no loving fathers abandon their children, and no stay-at-home dads abandon their children.

3. All first-degree murderers are felons. Consequently, <u>some first-degree murderers are thieves</u>, because some felons are thieves.

4. All categorical syllogisms are logical arguments, and all logical arguments are things made up of words. Thus, <u>some things made up of words are not categorical syllogisms.</u>

5. <u>Some quadrilaterals are squares,</u> for all rectangles are quadrilaterals, and all squares are rectangles.

6. <u>Some exogenous chemicals are synthesized from amino acids</u>, since no neurotransmitters are exogenous chemicals, and some neurotransmitters are synthesized from amino acids.

7. No Shakespearian dramas are epic poems, but some Shakespearian dramas are histories. Therefore, <u>some histories are not epic poems.</u>

8. All people who want to be continually reelected are career politicians, so <u>some pathological liars are not career politicians</u>, since no one who wants to be continually reelected is a pathological liar.

Problems 9–16: Determine whether the syllogism of the each of the problems above is valid or invalid. If it is invalid, explain the rule being broken.

9. #1 <u>Valid</u> _____

_____

10. #2 _Invalid. It has two negative premises (rule 2)._

11. #3 _Invalid. The middle term is not distributed in either premise (rule 3)._

12. #4 _Invalid. It has a negative conclusion, but two affirmative premises (rule 2)._

13. #5 _Valid_

14. #6 _Invalid. It has an affirmative conclusion, but a negative premise (rule 1)._

15. #7 _Valid_

16. #8 _Invalid. A term is distributed in the conclusion but not in its premise (rule 4)._

Problems 17–20: Develop a sound categorical syllogism with the given statement as the conclusion.   (Answers may vary)

17. All great speakers were once bad speakers.

   All unpracticed and ignorant speakers are bad speakers.
   All great speakers were once unpracticed and ignorant
   _   speakers._
   Therefore, all great speakers were once bad speakers.

18. No true freedom is truly free.

Nothing that comes at the price of opposing tyranny is truly
   free.
All true freedom comes at the price of opposing tyranny.
Therefore, no true freedom is truly free.

19. Some Jews are Christians.

All people who believe that Jesus is the promised Messiah are
   Christians.
Some Jews are people who believe that Jesus is the promised
   Messiah.
Therefore, some Jews are Christians.

20. Some words are not fit to speak.

All words that are fit to speak are kind.
Some words are not kind.
Therefore, some words are not fit to speak.

EXERCISE 22B

NAME

DATE

Problems 1–4: Write an enthymeme (complete proof) to establish the given conclusion. You may use the Aristotelian form "The fact that p is a sign that q" with the statement q as the conclusion. (Sample Answers)

1. "Your computer will eventually need to be replaced."

   The fact that your computer will become obsolete or break down is a sign that your computer will eventually need to be replaced.

2. "Texting during a theater performance is rude."

   Texting during a theater performance is rude because it will cause an unnecessary distraction to the people around you who are trying to enjoy the performance.

3. "Men are inclined to evil when justice is delayed."

   The fact that men do not expect to be punished when justice is delayed is a sign that they are inclined to evil when justice is delayed.

4. "True love does not fade with the beloved's absence."

   <u>True love does not fade with the beloved's absence, because</u>
   <u>with true love, absence simply makes the heart grow fonder.</u>

5. Write a refutable sign that could be used to support one of the conclusions from problems 1–4.

   <u>The fact that a timely execution of justice is a deterrent</u>
   <u>to evil is a sign that men are inclined to evil when justice is</u>
   <u>delayed.</u>

6. Write a valid disjunctive syllogism with this conclusion: "You should read the entire Bible."

   <u>You either read the entire Bible, or you remain ignorant about</u>
   <u>some of God's truth. You should not be ignorant about any of</u>
   <u>God's truth. Therefore, you should read the entire Bible.</u>

7. Write a pure hypothetical syllogism with this conclusion: "If you love your country, then you will fight to defend it."

   <u>If you love your country, then it is like your mother. If your</u>
   <u>country is like your mother, then you will fight to defend it.</u>
   <u>Therefore, if you love your country then you will fight to</u>
   <u>defend it.</u>

8. Write a *modus ponens* with this conclusion: "Stories are an effective means of teaching."

    If the Lord Jesus used stories to teach, then they must be an effective means of teaching. In his parables, Jesus used stories to teach. Therefore, stories are an effective means of teaching.

9. Write a *modus tollens* with this conclusion: "Christians should not worry about the future."

    If you worry about the future, then you are not trusting God to be good. But God has promised His children that He will be good to them. Therefore, Christians should not worry about the future.

10. Write a dilemma about deciding whether or not to buy a car.

    If I don't buy a car, then I have to keep borrowing my parents' car when I need to get somewhere. But if I buy a car, then I will use all the money I have saved. I either buy a car, or I do not. So either I have to regularly borrow my parents' car, or I have to use up all the money that I have saved.

11. Write a detailed argument on any topic. Include 1) a disjunctive syllogism, 2) a pure hypothetical syllogism, 3) a *modus ponens*, and 4) a *modus tollens*. Identify each by number in the margin.

Either God can learn, or He cannot. One can only learn something that one does not yet know. Hence, if God can learn, then He also must learn what He does not yet know. But if God learns what He does not know, then He is limited in wisdom (for without total knowledge there cannot be total wisdom). Therefore, if God can learn, then He is limited in wisdom. But God is not limited in wisdom, for the Scripture says, "Oh, the depth of the riches both of the wisdom and knowledge of God! How unsearchable are His judgments and His ways past finding out!" (Rom. 11:33). Hence, it is clear that God cannot learn. Now, if God cannot learn, then either He is limited in wisdom (for inability to learn can be due to a lack of wisdom) or He is omniscient (and already knows all things). But, as was just shown, God cannot learn. Thus He is limited in wisdom or He is omniscient. But it was already acknowledged that God is not limited in wisdom. Therefore, God is omniscient. (Sample Answer)

(2)

(4)

(3)

(1)

EXERCISE 23A

NAME

DATE

Problems 1–2: Section 1 of the Fourteenth Amendment to the U.S. Constitution reads,

> All persons born or naturalized in the United States, and subject to the jurisdiction thereof, are citizens of the United States and of the State wherein they reside. No State shall make or enforce any law which shall abridge the privileges or immunities of citizens of the United States; *nor shall any State deprive any person of life, liberty, or property, without due process of law;* nor deny to any person within its jurisdiction the equal protection of the laws.

In *Roe v. Wade*, the court decided that the Fourteenth Amendment's use of the word *person* did not refer to the unborn, and that, therefore, a fetus has no constitutional right to life.

1. What definition could be given for the word *person* that is consistent with the court's decision in *Roe v. Wade*? (You may do some research to help answer this question.)

   <u>A person is a human who has either been born or is unborn</u>
   <u>but is able to survive outside of the womb.</u>

2. Define the word *person* in a way that could be used to refute the court's decision.

   <u>A person is a human from the point of conception onward,</u>
   <u>having his own unique genetic makeup, able to be known by</u>
   <u>God as he forms in the womb (Psalm 139:13–16).</u>

Problems 3–4: Read Patrick Henry's "Give Me Liberty" speech, and answer the questions.

3. Henry apparently refutes the following objection: "We should continue to petition the British ministry. They gave our recent petition a gracious reception." Summarize Henry's two distinct refutations to this objection.

First, any gracious reception of our petitions is inconsistent with the military accumulation on our land and sea, which are all intended to force us into submission—there is no other reasonable explanation for their presence. Second, we have petitioned the British government for ten years in every possible way and have been repeatedly spurned. There is no longer any hope that Britain will listen to further petitions.

4. Henry then refutes this objection: "We are weak. We could not win a war against Britain." Summarize Henry's refutation to this objection.

We are not weak if we put forth the strength that we have without further delay. Consider our population of three million people armed in the cause of liberty. And the sovereign God will raise up allies in the battle.

5. During Absalom's rebellion in 2 Samuel 17, Ahithophel counsels Absalom to attack David at once (vv. 1–3), but Hushai counsels him to wait (vv. 8–13). Identify two key arguments by probability they use that completely differ between them.

    Ahithophel argues that David and his men are weary and discouraged and would flee if attacked. Hushai, on the contrary, argues that David and his men are mighty, angry, and crafty. They would kill some of Absalom's men when the fighting started, and then the rest of his people would flee.

6. In 2 Kings 19:10–13, the Rabshakeh of the king of Assyria uses an inductive argument to try to persuade King Hezekiah that the Lord cannot save Jerusalem. Summarize the argument, and explain why it is a weak argument (consider verses 15–19).

    The Rabshakeh argues that the gods of the other nations Assyria has attacked have been powerless to rescue them, so the Lord will similarly be unable to rescue Jerusalem. The argument is weak, not because of too few examples, or examples which are exceptions, but because the examples are not relevant to the conclusion. The gods of the nations are not gods, but idols. The Lord is the true God.

EXERCISE 23B

NAME

DATE

Problems 1–8: Identify the conditional argument as *modus ponens* (MP), *modus tollens* (MT), affirming the consequent (AC), or denying the antecedent (DA). You may abbreviate.

1. If you do well, then your sacrifice will be accepted. But Cain did not do well. Consequently, his sacrifice was not accepted.   DA

2. If I ascend into heaven, God is there. God is in heaven. Therefore, I have ascended into heaven.   AC

3. If ten righteous men had been found, then the city would have been spared. The city was not spared, so ten righteous men must not have been found.   MT

4. When the child was born a boy, he was to be killed. Moses was a son. Thus, Moses was to be killed.   MP

5. If a thief is caught, then he is to restore double. That child was caught stealing, so she had to restore double.   MP

6. If you want to live a godly life, then you will be persecuted. My friends and I are often persecuted. We must want to live godly lives.   AC

7. If a ruler listens to lies, then all of his servants become wicked. Many of Solomon's servants were not wicked. Clearly, he did not listen to lies.   MT

8. Mormon doctrine is true only if the Scripture mentions a third heaven. The Bible does mention a third heaven. Hence, Mormon doctrine is true.   AC

Problems 9–13: Refute the given dilemma. Identify the method used: grasping the horns, going between the horns, or rebutting the horns. Use each of these three methods at least once.   (Answers may vary)

9. If I try to teach a lot of concepts, then the lessons will be shallow. But if I try to teach only a few concepts, then I will not cover the subject completely. I try to teach a lot of concepts or only a few. Thus, my teaching is either shallow of incomplete.

    But if you teach a lot of concepts then you will cover more
    material. And if you teach a few concepts, then you will get to
    cover them deeply. You cover a lot of concepts or a few, so
    your teaching will be either deep or complete.

    Name the method used: Rebutting the horns

10. If people are good, then laws are not needed to prevent wrongdoing, but if people are evil, then the laws are not able to prevent wrongdoing. People are either good or evil. Consequently, laws are either not needed or not able to prevent wrongdoing.

    Laws that are enforced can help to prevent wrongdoing. Evil
    men will be more likely to avoid crime if they believe that
    punishment will be swift and painful.

    Name the method used: Grasping the horns

11. If the U.S. reduces carbon emissions, then our economy will be hampered. If we do not reduce carbon emissions, then we contribute to global warming. We either reduce carbon emissions or not, so either our economy is hampered or we contribute to global warming.

Even if we do not reduce carbon emissions, we will still not
contribute to global warming. Carbon emissions do not have as
big an impact on the temperature of our atmosphere as has
been suggested.

Name the method used: _Grasping the horns_

12. If Christians immerse themselves in modern culture, then they will be polluted by it. But for Christians to escape modern culture they must become hermits. Christians will either immerse themselves in modern culture or seek to escape it, so they will either be polluted by culture or they will become hermits.

We need neither fully immerse ourselves in modern culture nor
completely escape it. We can learn about modern culture and
how to interact with it in godly wisdom, and then work to
impact culture for the good of the kingdom.

Name the method used: _Going between the horns_

13. If you love someone, then you will hurt them, and if you love no one, then
    you will be lonely. You will love someone or no one, so you will hurt someone
    or you will be lonely.

    <u>It is not always true that if you love someone you will hurt</u>
    <u>them—not if you love them with a Christlike love that puts</u>
    <u>their interests ahead of your own.</u>

    Name the method used: <u>Grasping the horns</u>

Problems 14–18: Write a counterexample to the given syllogism or enthymeme. Make
sure that your premises are clearly true and that your conclusion is clearly false.
(Answers may vary)

14. All good poems rhyme, for all Shakespeare's sonnets are good poems, and
    all of them rhyme.

    <u>All poems are written by Shakespeare, for all Shakespeare's</u>
    <u>sonnets are poems, and all of Shakespeare's sonnets were</u>
    <u>written by Shakespeare.</u>

15. All formaldehyde-based laminates emit unhealthy gases, but some lami-
    nates are not formaldehyde based. Therefore, some laminates don't emit
    unhealthy gases.

    <u>All Formula 1 racecars use fuel, but some Lamborghinis are not</u>
    <u>Formula 1 race cars. Therefore, some Lamborghinis do not use</u>
    <u>fuel.</u>

16. No writers of lewd articles are decent citizens, but some journalists are not writers of lewd articles. Therefore, some journalists are decent citizens.

    No writers of lewd articles are digital clocks, but some journalists are not writers of lewd articles. Does that mean that some journalists are digital clocks?

17. Teenagers are not yet adults, because teenagers go to movies regularly.

    By that reasoning, movie critics must not be adults, because movie critics go to movies regularly.

18. Oswald must have been the lone assassin of Kennedy. After all, it's been over fifty years and nobody has proven that anyone else helped him.

    Oswald must have been part of a Russian conspiracy to murder Kennedy. After all, it's been over thirty years and nobody has proven that he worked alone without the Russians.

Problems 19–20: Write a *reductio ad absurdum* argument to refute the given claim.

19. If you die when you are dreaming, then you die in reality and never wake up.

    Let's assume that this is true, and that everyone who has dreamt that he or she died actually died before they woke. How then could we know this to be true? Who would be able to then report that they died in their sleep?

20. Words cannot convey meaning.

<u>If such were the case, then this sentence would have no</u>
<u>meaning. So if this claim is true, then it is meaningless. And if</u>
<u>it is false, and words do convey meaning, then it is wrong.</u>

_____

_____

EXERCISE 24A

NAME

DATE

Explain what the two fallacies have in common, then explain how they differ.

1. Bandwagon fallacy / *Ad misericordiam*

   Both fallacies are species of *ad populum,* appealing to the emotions of the masses. But the bandwagon fallacy relates more to appealing to the masses, and *ad misericordiam* relates more to appealing to the emotions.

2. False analogy / Straw man

   Both fallacies involve mischaracterization in argument. False analogy mischaracterizes a comparison to draw a false conclusion—an error in proof. The straw man mischaracterizes a position on some issue and then attacks that position—an error in refutation.

3. Hasty generalization / Composition

   Both fallacies argue from part to whole. Hasty generalization takes an attribute of one member (or few members) of a category and blindly applies it to the entire category. Composition looks at each and every part of a thing and applies the attributes of the parts to the thing as a whole, not in a "blind" manner.

4. Equivocation / Amphiboly

Both are fallacies of ambiguity, and both involve changing the meanings of words. Equivocation uses two different meanings of an ambiguous word to draw a wrong conclusion. Amphiboly depends not on ambiguous words, but ambiguous grammar.

5. Cherry-picking / Accident

Both fallacies move between generalizations and unrepresentative instances. Accident starts with a general rule and applies it to a specific case not covered by that rule. Cherry-picking (a species of hasty generalization) starts with an unrepresentative specific case and applies it generally. Hasty generalization is sometimes called converse accident.

EXERCISE 24B

NAME

DATE

Identify the informal fallacy being made. Be specific.

1. "No individual vote in an election makes a worthwhile difference, so elections are a worthless means of making public choices."

    <u>Composition</u>

2. "A large percentage of the voting public report that they plan to vote for Senator West, so she is clearly the best candidate."

    <u>Bandwagon fallacy (ad populum)</u>

3. "We wanted to hear from the student body about fun activities, so we asked the senior girls, and they all said we should have a formal dance. So that's what we should do."

    <u>Cherry-picking (hasty generalization)</u>

4. "You think that the school should have a formal dance just because you are a dance instructor!"

    <u>Bulverism (circumstantial ad hominem)</u>

5. "My sister says I shouldn't flirt with the lifeguard at the pool, but I have seen her talking with the guys at the café, so why should I listen to her?"

    <u>Tu quoque (ad hominem)</u>

6. "What's wrong with flirting with that lifeguard? Swimming is a healthy activity, and should get me in shape for running cross country!"

    <u>Red herring (missing the point)</u>

7. "Yes, officer, I know about the ordinance not to leave dogs in a car in hot weather. But I wasn't *leaving* my dog, I was just going into the store and then coming back."

   Accent

8. "Officer, it wouldn't be right to fine me for leaving my dog. I have had such a hard day, my husband yelled at me this morning, my son has the flu, and it's my birthday!"

   Ad misericordiam

9. "Why should we be confident that there is intelligent life on other planets? Because that biologist said so, and he even advocates trying to communicate with them."

   Ad verecundiam

10. "You don't think that there are intelligent aliens in our galaxy? You must believe that earth is the only planet where biological life can exist!"

    Either-or

11. "No one has proven that there is extraterrestrial life, so humans must indeed be alone."

    Ad ignorantiam

12. "The teachers at that college are all liberals, so when you go there to study, don't believe anything they say to you!"

    Poisoning the well (ad hominem, abusive)

13. "My daughter's first year of college cost $18,000, and for what? English 101, a philosophy course, and an easy math class. Higher education is a waste of time and money!"

    Hasty generalization

14. "The human body is like a machine, and it's not wrong to turn off a machine after it's been running a long time. So it is acceptable to end the life of the sick and aged."

<u>False analogy</u>

15. "If you continue advocating for death with dignity, some day you will be in a nursing home on life support, and they will end your life with no dignity at all!"

<u>Ad baculum</u>

16. "You shouldn't play poker with chips. Next thing you know you'll be playing for money, then playing at the casino, then losing all you have until you are on the streets begging!"

<u>Slippery slope</u>

17. "What's wrong with people begging? You are begging me to stop gambling!"

<u>Equivocation</u>

18. "Fathers should help their children with their studies, so I wrote my son's essay for him."

<u>Accident</u>

19. "Having students write thesis papers and defend them is a medieval practice that is not necessary in these modern times."

<u>Chronological snobbery</u>

20. "It is morally wrong to use animals for medical testing. Imagine researchers gleefully injecting poisons into puppies, and poking their exposed brains just to see what happens!"

<u>Straw man (missing the point)</u>

21. "America should not have stopped sending men to the moon. The last Apollo mission came back in December 1972, and what happened? In January 1973 we got *Roe v. Wade*."

    Post hoc ergo propter hoc

22. "We should continue to send astronauts to the moon because it would be beneficial for men to travel to the lunar surface."

    Begging the question

23. "You say I should learn good conversation skills because they will help me to be a good friend and to gain confidence. But there is so much more to learn: personal finances, auto repair, biblical Greek…"

    Ignoratio elenchi (missing the point)

24. "I have heard that learning biblical Greek will take years of intensive study, so it will probably take a long time to learn the Greek alphabet."

    Division

25. "A sign in the park read, 'If your dog messes on the grass, please dispose of it.' That sounds pretty harsh."

    Amphiboly

26. "Have you stopped abusing your dog?"

    Complex question

EXERCISE 25A

NAME

DATE

1. From the list of characteristics of the young versus the old, what emotion do you think would be the easiest to raise in young men? In old men? Briefly explain your answers.

   Anger, because young men are hot tempered and apt to give
   way to anger.
   Fear, because old men are cowardly, always anticipating
   danger. (Answers may vary.)

2. Write two paragraphs urging this thesis: "Every man should own a truck." Aim the first paragraph at young men and the second paragraph at old men.

   Young men: Do you want to have fun, make some money,
   and impress that special girl by being a hero? Then you
   should own a truck! A truck is a symbol of strength and
   independence. When your friend's little car gets stuck in a
   ditch, you and your truck can pull him out. With your truck
   you can help people move, haul stuff, and do yard work—
   earning you some extra cash. Are you and your friends
   planning a camping trip? You can be the guy to offer to
   carry all the bags and equipment. Do your buddies need a
   ride to the football game? Imagine taking them there with
   your lady at your side, and all your friends having fun in the
   back of your truck. A truck is the ticket to the life you look
   forward to!
       Older men: Looking back, do you remember all those times

when you had to transport furniture, haul away a dead tree, or move the equipment to and from your daughter's wedding? What did you have to do? You had to borrow a friend's truck. Or you had to spend money to rent a truck. What an inconvenience and what an unnecessary expense! You shouldn't have to keep dealing with such nonsense. Instead, you should buy a truck. It doesn't have to be a new one, just something that can move stuff from point A to point B. When things go wrong, as you know they eventually will, you might be able to fix it with a truck. A truck will help you serve your family and others in many ways, without being a burden to anyone else. In the long run, a truck is a good value. (Sample Answer)

3. Write two paragraphs urging this thesis: "Parents should begin saving money for their children from birth." Aim the first paragraph at men, and the second paragraph at women.

> Men: Saving money for your children from the day they are born is one of the wisest decisions you can ever make. Starting a fund for them right away will give that investment a lifetime to grow, and when your children are ready for college, they will know how well you have provided for their future security and will thank you for looking out for them. When others are scrambling to figure out how to pay for their kids' needs, you and your wife will be confident, because of the decision you made years before. Also, if you start right away, you can invest that money in a riskier fund with a greater likelihood of larger returns. Think it over, and you will see the benefits of investing early for your children.
>
> Women: Providing for your children's future financial needs from the day they are born is one of the most loving decisions you can ever make. Imagine the look of delight on your daughter's face when she learns that the beautiful wedding she always dreamed of is already paid for. Imagine your son's happiness when he discovers that he can provide better for his new wife because you started things off right. Your secure investment now provides for a secure future for them. Talk it over with your husband, or check with your financial advisor. They will agree that saving early is a smart choice. (Sample Answer)

_____

_____

_____

_____

_____

_____

_____

_____

_____

_____

EXERCISE 25B

NAME

DATE

1. Write two paragraphs arguing on one side or the other of this debate resolution: "It is right to keep animals in zoos." In the first paragraph, argue as a Christian, and the second paragraph, argue as an atheist.

Christian: It is right to keep animals in zoos. The Scriptures clearly teach that mankind has been made lord of the animals: "Let them have dominion over the fish of the sea, over the birds of the air, and over the cattle, over all the earth and over every creeping thing that creeps on the earth" (Gen. 1:26). We have been given charge over animals both to care for them and to use them for the benefit of all. Zoos can help us to do this. Zoos allow us to protect and preserve animals, especially endangered ones, just as God used Noah's ark to preserve all animals in the Flood. We can also learn about animals by observing them and reading about them in the zoo. Indeed, the education of young children alone is a worthy reason to keep animals in zoos. But animals should be given a comfortable environment, and be properly fed and cared for, as we read, "A righteous man regards the life of his animal" (Prov. 12:10).

   Atheist: It is cruel to keep animals in zoos, removing them from their native habitat and imprisoning them in cages, or at best maintaining them in a strange environment. Zoos cannot provide animals with their natural surroundings, diet, or proper socialization with their own kind. Humans are not somehow special, despite what we may think. We are no different from animals, and thus have no right to keep them locked up. Indeed, to exhibit animals in zoos is akin to giving tours of prisons for people to gawk at the inmates. Science has shown that animals feel and think much like we do. We share the earth with them, and thus we may not lord it over them as tyrants. The animals do not need us, and would be best provided for by simply being left in their homes in the wild. (Sample Answer)

EXERCISE 26A

NAME

DATE

Problems 1–3: Circle the nominalizations in the given sentences. Then improve their clarity by rewriting the sentences, turning nominalizations into their corresponding verbs and adjectives.

1. My father did his (work) for many hours of (thanklessness) in order to make (provision) for us.

   My father worked many thankless hours to provide for us.

2. Your (inability) to mount an (attack) against the Republic was due to the (prevention) of my guards.

   My guards prevented you from attacking the Republic.

3. The (expense) is significant for the (construction) and (maintenance) of power plants for the (harnessing) of wind energy.

   Power plants that harness wind energy are expensive to construct and maintain.

4. Use appropriate nominalizations to make this sentence shorter and clearer: "The fact that he completely understood the situation helped him to be particularly insightful."

   His complete understanding of the situation gave him particular insight.

Problems 5–6: Read the following excerpt from Patrick Henry's "Give Me Liberty" (line numbers have been added):

> [1] Sir, we have done everything that could be done to avert the storm which is now coming on. [2] We have petitioned; we have remonstrated; we have supplicated; we have prostrated ourselves before the throne, and have implored its interposition to arrest the tyrannical hands of the ministry and Parliament. [3] Our petitions have been slighted; our remonstrances have produced additional violence and insult; our supplications have been disregarded; and we have been spurned, with contempt, from the foot of the throne! [4] In vain, after these things, may we indulge the fond hope of peace and reconciliation.

5. In line 2, Henry gives us a series of four statements regarding what the colonists have done, balanced in line 3 by four statements about the response of the king. Write out the statements with the corresponding acts of the colonists and responses of the king placed side by side.

    We have petitioned—Our petitions have been slighted

    We have remonstrated—Our remonstrances have produced
      additional violence and insult

    We have supplicated—Our supplications have been disregarded

    We have prostrated ourselves before the throne—We have
      been spurned, with contempt, from the foot of the throne.

6. Which voice, active or passive, is used to describe the actions of the colonists? Which is used to describe the response of the king? Explain why Henry used each voice as he did.

    The active voice is used to describe the actions of the
    colonists, and the passive voice is used for the response of the
    king. This change of voice allows the point of view to remain

<u>on the colonists—the repeated efforts the colonists have</u>
<u>made and the dismissive response the colonists have suffered.</u>

Problems 7–8: Read this excerpt from Martin Luther King Jr.'s Letter from Birmingham Jail:

> So I have not said to my people: 'Get rid of your discontent.' Rather, I have tried to say that this normal and healthy discontent can be channeled into the creative outlet of nonviolent direct action. And now this approach is being termed extremist.

7. The second and third sentences use the passive voice. Rewrite the whole section with every sentence being grammatically active (you will have to invent reasonable agents of the action).

   <u>So I have not said to my people: 'Get rid of your discontent.'</u>
   <u>Rather, I have tried to say that they can channel this normal</u>
   <u>and healthy discontent into the creative outlet of nonviolent</u>
   <u>direct action. And now people such as you are claiming that</u>
   <u>this approach is extremist.</u>

8. Explain why the passive is the better choice for those sentences.

   <u>The passive voice allows the thoughts to be connected in a</u>
   <u>chain to maintain a proper flow of thought. The "discontent"</u>
   <u>at the end of the first sentence connects to the "normal and</u>
   <u>healthy discontent" at the beginning of the second. Also, the</u>

"nonviolent direct action" at the end of the second sentence connects with "this approach" that opens the third.

EXERCISE 26B

NAME

DATE

1. Rewrite this closing line of John F. Kennedy's Inaugural Address, removing as much as possible the rhythm and parallel structure.

> With a good conscience our only sure reward, with history the final judge of our deeds, let us go forth to lead the land we love, asking His blessing and His help, but knowing that here on earth God's work must truly be our own.

A good conscience is the only reward we are certain of, and the last judge of our deeds is history, so let us continue forward to lead this nation that we love, asking the blessings and the help of God, knowing that while we are on the earth we must truly do His work.

Problems 2–3: Follow the pattern of the analysis from the example at the end of the lesson to display the elegant structure of the given closing sentences. Because you will need extra room to maneuver, the questions are sideways on the next two pages.

2. "In short they have no refuge, nothing to take hold of; all that preserves them every moment is the mere arbitrary will, and uncovenanted, unobliged forbearance of an incensed God."

Diagram text:

In short they have { no refuge, / nothing to take hold of }

all that preserves them every moment is the { mere arbitrary will and { uncovenanted, unobliged } forbearance }

of an incensed God.

3. "If, then, I am not convinced by proof from Holy Scripture, or by cogent reasons, if I am not satisfied by the very text I have cited, and if my judgment is not in this way brought into subjection to God's word, I neither can nor will retract anything; for it cannot be right for a Christian to speak against his conscience."

If, then, I am not convinced

    by proof from Holy Scripture,

    or □,

    by cogent reasons

and

if I am not satisfied by the very text I have cited,

if my judgment is not in this way brought into subjection to God's word,

I neither can □

    nor retract anything.

    will □

for it cannot be right for a Christian to speak against his conscience.

EXERCISE 27A

NAME

DATE

Identify three figures of speech used in each of the given speech excerpts. Briefly explain each one to demonstrate your understanding of the figure.

1. "We Americans are vitally concerned in your defense of freedom. We are putting forth our energies, our resources, and our organizing powers to give you the strength to regain and maintain a free world. We shall send you in ever-increasing numbers, ships, planes, tanks, guns. That is our purpose and our pledge."—FDR, *Four Freedoms*

Anaphora: The first three sentences start with "we."

Asyndeton: The third sentence ends "planes, tanks, guns" rather than "and guns."

Alliteration: The last sentence connects the concepts of "purpose" and "pledge" with the initial consonant p. Also assonance with "strength" and "regain" and "maintain."

Climax: The phrase "our energies, our resources, and our organizing powers."

2. "Now is the time to make real the promises of democracy. Now is the time to rise from the dark and desolate valley of segregation to the sunlit path of racial justice. Now is the time to lift our nation from the quicksands of racial injustice to the solid rock of brotherhood. Now is the time to make justice a reality for all of God's children."—MLK, *I Have a Dream*

    Anaphora: The repeated "now is the time" at the beginning of each sentence.

    Antithesis: The two contrasting pairs in parallel structure— first, "the dark and desolate valley of segregation" and "the sunlit path of racial justice"; second, "the quicksands of racial injustice" and "the solid rock of brotherhood."

    Alliteration: The words "dark" and "desolate" are connected with the initial d. Also assonance with "solid" and "rock" and "brotherhood."

3. "So let us begin anew—remembering on both sides that civility is not a sign of weakness, and sincerity is always subject to proof. Let us never negotiate out of fear. But let us never fear to negotiate. Let both sides explore what problems unite us instead of belaboring those problems which divide us."— JFK, *Inaugural Address*

    Parallelism: The similar structure between "civility is not a sign of weakness" and "sincerity is always subject to proof."

    Antimetabole: The reverse order of "negotiate out of fear" and "fear to negotiate."

    Antithesis: The contrast between "what problems unite us" and "those problems which divide us."

4. "And we know that all things work together for good to those who love God, to those who are the called according to His purpose. For whom He foreknew, He also predestined to be conformed to the image of His Son, that He might be the firstborn among many brethren. Moreover whom He predestined, these He also called; whom He called, these He also justified; and whom He justified, these He also glorified. What then shall we say to these things? If God is for us, who can be against us?"—Romans 8:28–31

Anadiplosis: The chain of thoughts connecting the predestined, the called, the justified, and the glorified.

Anaphora: The successive clauses in the first sentence starting with "to those who."

Epistrophe: The successive clauses in the last sentence ending in "us."

5. "I have but one lamp by which my feet are guided, and that is the lamp of experience. I know of no way of judging of the future but by the past. And judging by the past, I wish to know what there has been in the conduct of the British ministry for the last ten years to justify those hopes with which gentlemen have been pleased to solace themselves and the House."—Patrick Henry, *Give Me Liberty*

Anaphora: The successive clauses in the first sentence starting with the word "lamp."

Antithesis: The contrast of "of the future" and "by the past."

Anadiplosis: The second and third sentences connected by "judging by the past."

6. "This day is called the feast of Crispian.
    He that outlives this day and comes safe home
    Will stand a tip-toe when the day is named
    And rouse him at the name of Crispian.
    He that shall live this day and see old age
    Will yearly on the vigil feast his neighbors,
    And say 'Tomorrow is Saint Crispian.'
    Then will he strip his sleeve and show his scars
    And say 'These wounds I had on Crispin's day.'
    Old men forget: yet all shall be forgot,
    But he'll remember with advantages
    What feats he did that day."
    —Henry V, *St. Crispin's Day*

<u>Isocolon:</u> Two similar isocolons in the second and third
   sentences: "outlives this day and comes safe home"; "live this
   day and see old age."

<u>Alliteration:</u> The repeated s sound in "strip his sleeve and show
   his scars and say."

<u>Antithesis:</u> The contrasting "Old men forget: yet all shall be
   forgot" and "but he'll remember."

EXERCISE 27B

NAME

DATE

Problems 1–5: Identify the primary figure of speech used in the given sentences. Then rewrite them in plain style, removing the figure of speech.

1. "The tablets were written on both sides; on the one side and on the other they were written. Now the tablets were the work of God, and the writing was the writing of God engraved on the tablets." (Exodus 32:15–16)

   Antimetabole.

   God engraved the writing on both sides of the tablets.

2. "...mankind are more disposed to suffer, while evils are sufferable, than to right themselves by abolishing the forms to which they are accustomed."— Declaration of Independence

   Polyptoton

   ...mankind are more disposed to suffer while they can, than to right themselves by abolishing the forms to which they are accustomed.

3. "You shall love the Lord your God with all your heart, with all your soul, with all your strength, and with all your mind." (Luke 10:27)

   Anaphora.

   You shall love the Lord your God with all your heart, soul, strength, and mind.

4. "Bishops air their opinions about economics; biologists, about metaphysics;
    inorganic chemists, about theology."—Sayers, *The Lost Tools of Learning*

    Zeugma.

    Bishops air their opinions about economics, biologists discuss
    metaphysics, and inorganic chemists talk about theology.

5. "And the kings of the earth, and the great men, and the rich men, and
    the chief captains, and the mighty men, and every bondman, and every
    free man, hid themselves in the dens and in the rocks of the mountains."
    (Revelation 6:15)

    Polysyndeton.

    Men of every station in life hid themselves in the mountains.

Problems 6–12: Rewrite or expand this sentence using a different figure of
speech from this lesson each time. Identify the figure used. Be creative!

    John climbed up the ladder in order to fix the leak in his roof.
    (Sample Answers)

6. John climbed the ladder, found the leak, and fixed the roof.
    (Isocolon)

7. John climbed up his sturdy, reliable ladder, and bent down to
    repair his unreliable roof.
    (Antithesis)

8. He climbed the ladder, fixed the leak, did his duty.
    (Asyndeton)

9. He climbed the ladder, he fixed the leak, and he made his wife
    proud.
    (Anaphora)

10. John zipped up his ladder and his roof.
    (Zeugma)

11. John climbed up the ladder—I had to lend him mine—in
    order to fix the leak in his roof.
    (Parenthesis)

12. Rickety ladders and leaky roofs are John's lot in life
    (Alliteration)

EXERCISE 28A

NAME

DATE

Problems 1–12: Identify the primary trope used in the given Bible verse. There is one each of the twelve tropes in the lesson.

1. "Would you plead for Baal? Would you save him? Let the one who would plead for him be put to death by morning!" (Judges 6:31)   *rhetorical question*

2. "They were swifter than eagles, they were stronger than lions." (2 Samuel 1:23)   *hyperbole*

3. "For I will not trust in my bow, nor shall my sword save me." (Psalm 44:6)   *synecdoche*

4. "Wisdom calls aloud outside; she raises her voice in the open squares." (Proverbs 1:20)   *personification*

5. "We are the clay, and You our potter; and all we are the work of Your hand." (Isaiah 64:8)   *metaphor*

6. "I have raised My hand in an oath that surely the nations that are around you shall bear their own shame. But you, O mountains of Israel, you shall shoot forth your branches and yield your fruit to My people Israel, for they are about to come." (Ezekiel 36:7–8)   *apostrophe*

7. "For where your treasure is, there your heart will be also." (Matthew 6:21)

    <u>metonymy</u>

8. "Behold, I send you out as sheep in the midst of wolves. Therefore be wise as serpents and harmless as doves." (Matthew 10:16)

    <u>simile</u>

9. "What shall I do? For my master is taking the stewardship away from me. I cannot dig; I am ashamed to beg." (Luke 16:3)

    <u>*dubitatio*</u>

10. "For you put up with fools gladly, since you yourselves are wise!" (2 Corinthians 11:19)

    <u>irony</u>

11. "For when I am weak, then I am strong." (2 Corinthians 12:10)

    <u>oxymoron</u>

12. "For God is not unjust to forget your work and labor of love which you have shown toward His name" (Hebrews 6:10)

    <u>litotes</u>

Problems 13–16: Identify three different figures of thought used in each of the given Bible passages. Briefly defend your answer.

13. "Where were you when I laid the foundations of the earth? Tell Me, if you have understanding. Who determined its measurements? Surely you know!" (Job 38:4–5)

    <u>Rhetorical questions—1st and 3rd sentences</u>
    <u>Irony—"Surely you know!"</u>
    <u>Metaphor—"foundations of the earth"</u>

14. "All flesh is grass, and all its loveliness is like the flower of the field." (Isaiah 40:6)

> Metaphor—"flesh is grass"
>
> Simile—"its loveliness is like the flower of the field"
>
> Synecdoche—"flesh" for mankind

15. "O Ephraim, what shall I do to you? O Judah, what shall I do to you? For your faithfulness is like a morning cloud, and like the early dew it goes away." (Hosea 6:4)

> Dubitatio–First two sentences (God speaking as if He does not
>
> know what to say)
>
> Rhetorical questions—1st and 2nd sentences
>
> Simile–"your faithfulness is like a morning cloud"

16. "You are already full! You are already rich! You have reigned as kings without us—and indeed I could wish you did reign, that we also might reign with you!" (1 Corinthians 4:8)

> Irony—"You are already full/rich"
>
> Simile and hyperbole—"You have reigned as kings."

Problems 17–20: Give the Bible reference for the verses alluded to in the given speech excerpts.

17. "I compelled to carry the gospel of freedom beyond my own home town. Like Paul, I must constantly respond to the Macedonian call for aid."— MLK, Letter from Birmingham Jail.

> Acts 16:9–10

18. "Now the trumpet summons us again … to bear the burden of a long twilight struggle, year in and year out, 'rejoicing in hope, patient in tribulation'—a struggle against the common enemies of man: tyranny, poverty, disease, and war itself." JFK, Inaugural Address.

Romans 12:12

19. "They know only the rules of a generation of self-seekers. They have no vision, and when there is no vision the people perish." FDR, First Inaugural Address.

Proverbs 29:18

20. "If they ask us here why it is we say more on the money question than we say upon the tariff question, I reply that if protection has slain its thousands the gold standard has slain its tens of thousands." William Jennings Bryan, Cross of Gold.

1 Samuel 18:7

EXERCISE 28B

NAME

DATE

Rewrite the sentences from Exercise 28a, problems 1–12, communicating the same information, but removing as much as possible any figures of thought.

1. You are pleading for Baal. You cannot save him. Let the one who would plead for him be put to death by morning!

2. They were very swift and very strong.

3. For I will not trust to save myself using my weapons.

4. Everyone has the opportunity to learn wisdom.

5. God created all of us.

6. I have taken an oath that surely the people of the nations that are around you shall be ashamed of themselves. But the mountains of Israel will be used to provide for the Israelites, for they are about to come.

7. For the location of your treasure will be the place that you are concerned about.

8. <u>I am sending you out among dangerous people. Therefore be wise but harmless.</u>

9. <u>I do not know what to do. For my master is taking the stewardship away from me. I cannot dig; I am ashamed to beg.</u>

10. <u>For you put up with fools, but you are not wise.</u>

11. <u>For when I am physically weak, then I am spiritually strong.</u>

12. <u>For God is just, so He will remember your work and the loving labor that you have shown toward Him.</u>

Problems 13–20: Rewrite or expand this sentence using a different figure of thought from the lesson for each answer. Identify the figure used. Be creative!

    It was very cold outside.
    (Sample Answers)

13. <u>Metaphor: "The cold night air was a scalpel slicing me to the bone."</u>

14. <u>Simile: "The icy wind penetrated my sweater like a steel dagger."</u>

15. <u>Metonymy: "I wanted to wear shorts outside today, but the</u>
    <u>weatherman was not my friend."</u>

    _____

16. <u>Personification: "The night air was a harsh task master,</u>
    <u>whipping me at every step."</u>

    _____

17. <u>*Dubitatio*: "I cannot begin to tell you how cold it was outside."</u>

    _____

18. <u>Hyperbole: "As I stepped outside, my breath turned to icicles,</u>
    <u>and I froze solid."</u>

    _____

19. <u>Rhetorical question: "Did you go outside? Did you feel how cold</u>
    <u>it was?"</u>

    _____

20. <u>Litotes: "I was not unaware that the temperature has fallen</u>
    <u>outside."</u>

    _____

21. Rewrite that same sentence again, using an allusion from a song, a story, or
    a poem.
    <u>"It was so cold outside I was wishing I could join Sam McGee</u>
    <u>in the boiler of the 'Alice May.'" (Sample answer)</u>

    _____

    _____

EXERCISE 29

NAME

DATE

1. Use the backgrounds and images given in the text to memorize the first portion of Hamlet's "To be or not to be" soliloquy.

> To be, or not to be? That is the question—
> Whether 'tis nobler in the mind to suffer
> The slings and arrows of outrageous fortune,
> Or to take arms against a sea of troubles,
> And, by opposing, end them? To die, to sleep—
> No more—and by a sleep to say we end
> The heartache and the thousand natural shocks
> That flesh is heir to—'tis a consummation
> Devoutly to be wished! To die, to sleep.
> To sleep, perchance to dream—ay, there's the rub,
> For in that sleep of death what dreams may come
> When we have shuffled off this mortal coil,
> Must give us pause. There's the respect
> That makes calamity of so long life.

2. Use the backgrounds and images method to memorize this next portion of Hamlet's "To be or not to be" soliloquy:

> For who would bear the whips and scorns of time,
> Th' oppressor's wrong, the proud man's contumely
> The pangs of despised love, the law's delay,
> The insolence of office, and the spurns
> That patient merit of th' unworthy takes,
> When he himself might his quietus make
> With a bare bodkin? Who would fardels bear,
> To grunt and sweat under a weary life,
> But that the dread of something after death,
> The undiscovered country, from whose bourn
> No traveller returns, puzzles the will,
> And makes us rather bear those ills we have
> Than fly to others that we know not of?

3. Use the repetition and removal method to memorize the last portion of Hamlet's "To be or not to be" soliloquy.

> Thus conscience does make cowards of us all,
> And thus the native hue of resolution
> Is sicklied o'er with the pale cast of thought,
> And enterprise of great pitch and moment
> With this regard their currents turn awry
> And lose the name of action.

EXERCISE 30A

NAME

DATE

Problems 1–9: For each given line, identify an emotion appropriate to it, and describe what could be done in regard to the elements of delivery to convey that emotion. Also circle any words that would be particularly emphasized (no more than a few each). (Answers may vary)

1. "What have you done, that you have (stolen) away unknown to me, and carried away my daughters like (captives) taken with the sword?"—Laban, Genesis 31:26

   Anger. Laban's voice would be louder, perhaps harsh, varying in
   tone at the emphasized words. Laban would look Jacob in the
   eye, frowning. He might walk right up to him. At "carried away
   my daughters" he could gesture with his arm toward them,
   palm upward.

2. "But now, do not therefore be grieved or angry with yourselves because you sold me here; for (God) sent me before you to preserve life."—Joseph, Genesis 45:5

   Calmness. Joseph's voice would be quiet and steady. He would
   look around at his brothers, perhaps with a slight, disarming
   smile. He might slightly shake his head, and hold up his hand,
   palm toward them at "do not therefore be grieved or angry
   with yourselves."

3. "Then(all)this assembly shall know that the Lord does(not)save with sword and spear; for the battle is the(Lord's,)and He will give you into our hands."—David, 1 Samuel 17:47

   <u>Confidence. David's voice would be loud, steady, and ringing</u>
   <u>with boldness. He would be raising himself up, looking directly</u>
   <u>at Goliath even as he gestures with his arm toward the army</u>
   <u>of Israel at "all this assembly."</u>

4. "For I say to you that(God)is able to raise up children to Abraham from these (stones.")—John the Baptist, Matthew 3:9

   <u>Indignation. John's voice would be loud and firm. He would not</u>
   <u>smile at his own bold claim, but would be looking around at the</u>
   <u>Pharisees and Sadducees. He might gesture with his arm out</u>
   <u>toward the stones, lifting it slightly at "raise up."</u>

5. "Together let us(explore)the stars,(conquer)the deserts,(eradicate)disease, (tap)the ocean depths, and(encourage)the arts and commerce."—John F. Kennedy, Inaugural Address

   <u>Friendship. Kennedy spoke with a peaceful confidence, with a</u>
   <u>steady voice, and upright posture. He used very few gestures.</u>

6. "You all did(love)him once, not without cause: / What cause withholds you then, to(mourn)for him?"—Mark Antony, Shakespeare's *Julius Caesar*

   <u>Pity. Antony is moving between anger and pity, so his voice</u>
   <u>would be louder than normal when seeking to raise pity. He</u>

would perhaps pause after "not without cause" to let his words sink in. His face would look grim. He might gesture with his arm toward Caesar's body at this line.

7. "Look, in this place ran (Cassius) dagger through. / See what a rent the envious (Casca) made. / Through this the well-beloved (Brutus) stabb'd."—Mark Antony, Shakespeare's *Julius Caesar*

Enmity. Antony's voice would be sad and stern. He would likely pause between each sentence, so that the hearers could think about what each conspirator did as he describes it. He might not look at his audience at all, but might be looking down sadly. He would gesture with his hand toward each hole in Caesar's robe.

8. "We (few,) we (happy) few, we band of (brothers.")—Henry V, St. Crispin's Day speech, Shakespeare's *Henry V*

Friendship. His voice would get quieter at this point, slightly pausing between each phrase for emphasis. He would look around at his men, perhaps smiling at them. He might gesture toward them with one or both hands, but not necessarily.

9. "We can (never) be satisfied as long as our children are (stripped) of their selfhood and (robbed) of their dignity by signs stating: 'For Whites only.'"—Martin Luther King Jr., "I Have a Dream"

Shame, anger. King spoke with a steady dignity, his voice loud
and resonant, and a little faster here to express his anger.
Emphasizing each of the last three words is appropriate. His
face would be stern as he looked around at his audience,
slightly gesturing with his head or arms toward them.

_____
_____
_____

Problems 10–14: Read the following verses. Identify the gestures that the speaker makes in each and the thoughts or feelings that their gestures are meant to convey.

10. 2 Kings 1:13   _The captain fell on his knees before Elijah, perhaps_
looking up at him with his hands clasped. He is trying to
convey his own humility and his fear of Elijah's power as well
as some pity toward him and his men.

_____
_____

11. Matthew 12:49   _Jesus stretched out his hand to his disciples_
(in Mark 3:34 he also looks around at them) indicating that
they who were with Him and doing the Father's will were His
family, rather than His natural family outside wanting Him to
come to them.

_____
_____
_____

12. Luke 18:13 <u>The tax collector looked down and beat his breast,</u>
<u>showing his shame and humble contrition at his sin.</u>
_____
_____

13. Acts 14:14 <u>Paul and Barnabas tore their clothes and ran in</u>
<u>among the multitude, expressing their grief at their idolatry</u>
<u>and trying to prevent them from sacrificing to them.</u>
_____
_____

14. Acts 21:40 <u>Paul motioned with his hand to the people, perhaps</u>
<u>stretching out his arm palm outward to quiet them and bid</u>
<u>them listen, which is what they do.</u>
_____
_____

EXERCISE 30B

NAME

DATE

Read through this introduction to Cicero's First Oration against Catiline. Describe on the lines to the right the various elements of delivery appropriate to that part of the speech. Include specific emotions and likely changes in voice, countenance, and gesture. (Answers may vary)

When, O Catiline, do you mean to cease abusing our patience? How long is that madness of yours still to mock us? When is there to be an end of that unbridled audacity of yours, swaggering about as it does now? Do not the nightly guards placed on the Palatine Hill—do not the watches posted throughout the city—does not the alarm of the people, and the union of all good men—does not the precaution taken of assembling the senate in this most defensible place—do not the looks and countenances of this venerable body here present, have any effect upon you? Do you not feel that your plans are detected? Do you not see that your conspiracy is already arrested and rendered powerless by the knowledge which everyone here

Cicero expresses enmity, anger, and indignation at the fact that Catiline dares to appear among them. His voice would be loud and expressive. He would look straight at him, with eyebrows contracted. He might gesture outside at these phrases.

Here he would gesture with his hands toward the other senators, or perhaps nod his heads toward them as he looked at Catiline.

161

possesses of it? What is there that you did last night, what the night before—where is it that you were—who was there that you summoned to meet you—what design was there which was adopted by you, with which you think that any one of us is unacquainted? Shame on the age and on its principles! The senate is aware of these things; the consul sees them; and yet this man lives. Lives! aye, he comes even into the senate. He takes a part in the public deliberations; he is watching and marking down and checking off for slaughter every individual among us. And we, gallant men that we are, think that we are doing our duty to the republic if we keep out of the way of his frenzied attacks.

With each of these phrases he might get increasingly louder, perhaps emphasizing the "what, where, who." He would be very loud on the word "shame" and its sentence and louder on the word "lives!" He might indicate the entrance. He would here look at the rest of the senators, perhaps gesturing toward them. At "every individual" he might look at specific persons.

WORKS CITED IN EXERCISES

In addition to the works cited in the main text, which are fully documented there, the following texts are used in this workbook.

Beckmann, Petr. "Newton." *A History of Pi*. New York: St. Martin's, 1976. 134–40. Print.

Bryan, William Jennings. "A Cross of Gold." Democratic National Convention, Chicago. 9 July 1896. Speech.

Grant, George. "An Unpopular Vision." Ligonier Ministries. *Tabletalk Magazine*, 1 Feb. 2010. Web. 11 May 2016.

King, Martin Luther, Jr. "Letter from Birmingham Jail," as published in *Gospel of Freedom*, Jonathan Rieder. New York: Bloomsbury Press, 2013. Print.

Roosevelt, Franklin D. "First Inaugural Address." U. S. Capitol, Washington D.C. 4 Mar. 1933. Speech.

Shakespeare, William. "Hamlet, Prince of Denmark." Act III, Scene 1. *Shakespeare II. Great Books of the Western World*. Ed. Mortimer Adler. Second ed. Vol. 25. Chicago: Encyclopedia Britannica, 1990. 47 Print.

Wilson, Woodrow. "War Speech." U.S. Congress, Washington D.C. 2 Apr. 1917. Speech.

EXAM ANSWER KEYS

The exams on the following pages are formatted identically to the ones in the exam packet. This layout will allow you to grade efficiently as you compare each student's paper with the answer key. Suggested point values are provided [in brackets].

EXAM ONE

LESSONS 1-4

NAME

DATE

You will need a Bible for this exam.

1. Define *rhetoric*.

   <u>Rhetoric is the art of persuasive speaking and writing. [2]</u>

2. List Cicero's three goals of rhetoric, showing how they relate to truth, goodness, and beauty.

   <u>To teach men the truth, to move men to goodness, and to</u>
   <u>delight men with beauty. [3]</u>

3. Give two Bible references where God is characterized as a *speaking* God.

   <u>Genesis 1:3, Psalm 33:6, Isaiah 46:10–11; 55:11, Hebrews 1:3 (any</u>
   <u>two; other passages may also be appropriate) [2]</u>

4. Give three Bible references where we are told to speak *righteously*. One reference must be from Proverbs and another from the New Testament.

   <u>Proverbs 10:19–21; 15:28; 25:11, Ecclesiastes 5:2–3, Matthew 12:33–</u>
   <u>35. (any three; other passages may also be appropriate) [3]</u>

5. Name two early philosophical rhetoricians.

   <u>Socrates, Plato, Aristotle, Cicero, Quintilian (any two) [2]</u>

6. Name a famous sophist. What characterized the rhetoric of the early sophists?

   <u>Gorgias, Protagoras, Thrasymachus, Prodicus, Hippias, Polus, Callicles</u>
   <u>(any one). The sophists were famous for delivering speeches in a</u>

poetic style, and taught by memorization and imitation. [4]

_____

_____

_____

_____

7. Write out *one* of the two Developing Memory quotes from the *Phaedrus* dialogue.

"The art of disputation, then, is not confined to the courts and the assembly, but is one and the same in every use of language; this is the art, if there be such an art, which is able to find a likeness of everything to which a likeness can be found, and draws into the light of day the likenesses and disguises which are used by others." OR "And this skill he will not attain without a great deal of trouble, which a good man ought to undergo, not for the sake of speaking and acting before men, but in order that he may be able to say what is acceptable to God and always to act acceptably to Him as far as in him lies." [6]

8. Summarize the story of the birth of technical rhetoric, including names, places, and years. Explain how the situation led to the writing of handbooks of rhetoric.

In 465 BC, the people of Syracuse deposed the tyrant Thrasybulus, who had ruled over them after his brother Hieron, and established a democracy after the pattern of Athens. The democracy included government by popular assembly and trial by jury. The citizens of Syracuse who wanted their private property restored to them sought justice through the courts of law, but since there were no professional lawyers to represent them, many found themselves unprepared to argue their own case. Some men named Corax and Tisias took advantage of this situation and taught the citizens of Syracuse rules for speaking in court. At first they taught orally, but later their teachings were written into handbooks. [9]

9. Summarize Socrates' criticisms of rhetoric from the *Phaedrus* dialogue.

According to Socrates, the rhetoricians of his day ignored truth, justice, goodness, and honor, and sought persuasion only through popular opinion. Rhetoric was not practiced as a universal art, but only in the courts and public assemblies. The rhetoricians were insincere, arguing on either side of a cause as it pleased them. They did not present their arguments in a proper order or arrangement. They were unable to define the nature of rhetoric, understanding only the preliminary conditions of it and maintaining that this made up the whole art. They did not base their proofs on facts or truth, but rather on probabilities. [9]

EXAM TWO

LESSONS 5-9

NAME

DATE

1. The first of the five faculties of oratory is invention. Define *invention*.

   "The devising of matter, true or plausible, that would make the case convincing." Invention is a means of developing arguments through creativity and experience. [2]

2. List the other four faculties of oratory.

   arrangement, style, memory, delivery [4]

3. Write a good thesis statement (to be used in problems 4–7).

   Christians are free to celebrate a traditional Christmas. (Sample. Answer must be a statement that is disputable, provable, clear, interesting, and embodying one idea.) [2]

Problems 4–7: For each problem, identify a different category of questions of stasis, then write one specific question of stasis based on the thesis statement from your answer to problem 3 along with a brief answer. [4 each]

4. Conjecture: Does a traditional celebration of Christmas exist? Yes, there are many common elements in the traditional celebration of Christmas: December 25, stories of Jesus' birth, singing carols, exchanging gifts, trees, lights, and enjoying feasts with family and friends.

5. <u>Definition: What kind of a thing is Christmas? Christmas is a</u>
<u>holiday, part of the traditional Christian calendar, not a "holy</u>
<u>day" in the sense that celebrating it is obligatory, but a day</u>
<u>which Christians are free to set aside to enjoy and remember</u>
<u>God's gift of Jesus Christ.</u>

6. <u>Quality: Is celebrating Christmas wise or foolish? It could be</u>
<u>approached foolishly, if people felt obligated to celebrate it or</u>
<u>if they celebrated it in a secular way centered on Santa and</u>
<u>shopping. But it can be a wise use of time to rejoice in God's</u>
<u>goodness through Jesus.</u>

7. <u>Policy: Should Christians celebrate a traditional Christmas?</u>
<u>Yes, they should think of it as something they are free to do,</u>
<u>rather than something they ought to do. They should use it</u>
<u>as an opportunity to publically celebrate the story of Jesus'</u>
<u>birth.</u>

8. According to the *Ad Herennium*, what are the purposes of an *introduction* to a speech?

<u>To make your audience receptive, well-disposed, and attentive.</u>
[3]

9. When is it rhetorically permissible or beneficial to skip the introduction to a speech?

   You may skip it if the audience is already receptive, well-disposed, and attentive, especially if the speech is short and the topic simple, or to show the urgency of the matter. [3]

10. Name five types of good introduction (other than skipping the introduction).

    Bid your hearers to listen, refer to the occasion or setting of the speech, refer to a previous speech, ask interesting questions, state something surprising, tell a story, or elaborate on a quote (any five). [5]

11. Identify several of the purposes of the *narration* of a speech.

    The narration prepares the audience for the proof, giving them the information they need, such as historical background, explaining the current situation, defining special terms, or anything else they need to understand the arguments to be presented. [4]

12. Describe the parts of the *division* of a speech.

    The first part is a statement clarifying the issues that you and your opponents agree upon and those that are disputed. The second part is an enumeration and preview of your proofs. [4]

_____

_____

_____

_____

13. Why should a speech usually not arrange proofs from the strongest down to the weakest?

If you follow that order, your speech will have a sense of deflating as it goes on, and will leave the weaker argument last, lingering in the minds of the audience. [3]

_____

_____

14. Explain how to effectively arrange arguments in the refutation to a speech.

Arguments of refutation should start by attacking your opponent's strongest arguments and end by dealing with his weakest. This shows that you are willing to meet his arguments head on and leaves his weakest arguments lingering in the hearer's minds. [3]

_____

_____

_____

15. Name five types of good conclusions to a speech.

Summarizing main points, calling the hearers to action, quoting a famous saying, contrasting yourself with your opponents, making a prediction, bookending (any five). [5]

_____

_____

EXAM THREE

LESSONS 10-13

NAME

DATE

1. List the three artistic modes of persuasion and explain what it means that they are *artistic*.

   <u>The three artistic modes of persuasion are ethos, pathos, and</u>
   <u>logos. They are artistic in that they must be invented by the</u>
   <u>speaker, who has to think of words to say to establish his</u>
   <u>own character, the audience's emotion, and the arguments in</u>
   <u>the speech. [4]</u>

2. Define *ethos*, and explain why it is helpful to establish ethos at the beginning of a speech.

   <u>Ethos is persuasion achieved by the personal character of the</u>
   <u>speaker. You should establish ethos at the beginning of your</u>
   <u>speech so that your audience will trust you as you move their</u>
   <u>emotions and believe you as you present your arguments. [4]</u>

3. Read the following introduction of Elihu's speech in Job 33:1–7. What are the three parts of invented ethos? What does Elihu say to establish each of the three parts for himself? Defend your answers.

   ¹ But please, Job, hear my speech, and listen to all my words. ² Now, I open my mouth; my tongue speaks in my mouth. ³ My words come from my upright heart; my lips utter pure knowledge. ⁴ The Spirit of God has made me, and the breath of the Almighty gives me life. ⁵ If you can answer me,

set your words in order before me; take your stand. ⁶ Truly I am as your spokesman before God; I also have been formed out of clay. ⁷ Surely no fear of me will terrify you, nor will my hand be heavy on you.

The three parts of invented ethos are good sense, good moral character, and good will toward one's hearers. Elihu shows or declares his good sense in verse 3, where he claims pure knowledge, and in verse 5, where he challenges Job to answer him. Elihu establishes good moral character when he claims in verse 3 that he is upright and pure. Elihu establishes his good will toward Job in verse 6 when he says that he is Job's spokesman and in verse 7 when he says that he will not terrify Job and that his hand will not be heavy on him. [9]

4. Define *copiousness*, and name two things a person can do to become more copious.

Copiousness is the idea of being full of true thoughts and wise words, having good things to say to benefit others. To become more copious, one can read great books, learn from wise people, expand life experiences, or keep a commonplace book (any two). [4]

5. What is Aristotle's definition of *emotions*?

Those feelings that so change men as to affect their judgments, and that are also attended by pain or pleasure. [3]

6. Define *pathos*, and defend the use of pathos in helping to persuade.

   <u>Pathos is persuasion achieved by putting the audience into a</u>
   <u>proper emotional frame of mind. God has made us to feel as</u>
   <u>well as to think, and we cannot separate our feelings from our</u>
   <u>decisions. When we persuade, we will make emotional appeals.</u>
   <u>The question is not whether people will try to influence</u>
   <u>others emotions in their speaking, but whether they will do</u>
   <u>so in a proper way, a way that is appropriate to the situation</u>
   <u>and pleasing to God. [6]</u>

Problems 7–10: Write Aristotle's definition of the given emotion. [3 each]

7. Anger <u>An impulse, accompanied by pain, to a conspicuous</u>
   <u>revenge for a conspicuous slight directed without justification</u>
   <u>towards what concerns oneself or towards what concerns</u>
   <u>one's friends.</u>

8. Fear <u>A pain or disturbance due to a mental picture of some</u>
   <u>destructive or painful evil in the future.</u>

9. Shame <u>Pain or disturbance in regard to bad things, whether</u>
   <u>past, present, or future, which seem likely to involve us in</u>
   <u>discredit.</u>

10. Pity A feeling of pain caused by the sight of some evil,
destructive or painful, which befalls one who does not deserve
it, and which we might expect to befall ourselves or some
friend of ours.

11. Which emotion is the opposite of *anger*? Calmness [1]

12. Which emotion is the opposite of *fear*? Confidence [1]

13. Which emotion is the opposite of *friendship*? Enmity [1]

14. Explain the primary difference between *pity* and *indignation*.

    Pity is pain caused by the sight of undeserved bad fortune,
    but indignation is pain caused by the sight of undeserved good
    fortune. The difference is the kind of fortune that the person
    being perceived is experiencing. [3]

15. Describe three specific differences between *anger* and *enmity*.

    Anger is produced by offenses against oneself; enmity might be
    produced just be what they perceive to be the other person's
    character. Anger is always felt toward specific persons; enmity
    may be felt toward whole classes of people. Anger is always
    accompanied by pain; enmity is not. Anger fades over time;
    enmity does not. (Any three) [6]

16. What is *emulation*? Toward whom do we feel emulation?

Aristotle defines emulation as pain caused by seeing the presence, in persons whose nature is like our own, of good things that are highly valued and are possible for ourselves to acquire. It is a good feeling felt by good people, a feeling that motivates us to take steps to become like someone we admire. We emulate people who have succeeded in gaining good things that we feel we have not. [6]

EXAM FOUR

LESSONS 14-16

NAME

DATE

You may use a Bible for this exam.

1. Define *forensic oratory*.

   <u>Speeches of accusation or defense, often given before a jury,</u>
   <u>concerned with the justice or injustice of someone's past</u>
   <u>actions [3]</u>

Problems 2–7: Consider this comic, which shows how Calvin followed an instruction to shovel a path to his father's car.

2. Define *wrongdoing*. Explain how Calvin's act fits each part of the definition.

   <u>Wrongdoing is "injury, voluntarily inflicted, contrary to law."</u>
   <u>Calvin's act was an injury in that his dad suffered harm</u>
   <u>(having to walk around a long path rather than a short one)</u>
   <u>against his will. It was voluntary (Calvin knew what he was</u>
   <u>doing, and no one was forcing him), and it was contrary to</u>
   <u>the implied command of his dad. [6]</u>

3. Is the law Calvin is breaking *universal* or *particular*? Explain your answer.

    The command to shovel a path from the porch to the car
    would be particular, but Calvin is clearly breaking a universal
    law of kindness: making things easier for others. [3]

4. What is Calvin's basic *state of mind* in doing this wrong?

    He would be found out, but either expected not to be punished
    (because his dad was in a hurry) or thought the gain from
    playing the trick on his dad outweighed the punishment. [3]

5. Briefly describe the *means, opportunity,* and *motive* for Calvin's wrong act.

    Means: Calvin had the shovel and the strength to dig that
    length of path.
    Opportunity: Calvin had the time to shovel the path, and was
    apparently doing so without being watched.
    Motive: Calvin perhaps gained pleasure from playing a trick on
    his dad (power over others). [6]

6. Why is Calvin's act here a greater wrongdoing than a typical act of disobedience?

    Calvin failed to fulfill an obligation, wronged a benefactor, is no
    doubt a repeat offender, and his act was especially deliberate.
    [2]

7. Which class of victims does Calvin's father fit under?

   <u>Calvin's dad was easy to wrong: he did not take precautions</u>
   <u>to supervise Calvin. He may have been pleasant to wrong, as</u>
   <u>Calvin may have had a grievance against him. [2]</u>

8. What is defined as "a sort of justice, applying to forgivable actions, that goes beyond the written law and makes up for defects in it"?

   <u>Equity [1]</u>

Problems 9–12: Imagine that you are trying to convince a group of friends to join a self-defense martial arts class with you this summer.

9. Appeal to the parts of the definition of *political oratory* to show this to be a political speech.

   <u>You are urging a group of people (your friends) to take a</u>
   <u>course of action (join the class with you) in the future (this</u>
   <u>summer), based on expediency (that they will benefit in some</u>
   <u>way). [4]</u>

10. To which of Aristotle's four definitions of *happiness* might you appeal to convince your friends? Explain.

    <u>"Good condition of property and body." If you learn martial</u>
    <u>arts, you can get in shape, defend yourself and others, and</u>
    <u>feel secure. (Answers may vary) [3]</u>

11. List four of Aristotle's constituent parts of happiness to which you could reasonably appeal.

   <u>Health, strength, athletic ability, good friends, and perhaps</u>
   <u>beauty and honor (any four). [4]</u>

12. To which of Aristotle's four definitions of *goodness* might you appeal? Explain.

   <u>"That which must be prescribed for a given individual by</u>
   <u>reason." You might argue that you have thought it through, and</u>
   <u>concluded that by choosing to join the martial arts class you</u>
   <u>will get the good things above (health, strength, etc.) (Answers</u>
   <u>may vary). [3]</u>

13. What is *ceremonial oratory*?

   <u>Speeches of praise or censure which are based upon honor or</u>
   <u>dishonor, requiring no decision from the hearers. [3]</u>

14. Two forms of virtue are *magnificence* and *liberality*. What do these virtues have in common? How do they differ?

   <u>Magnificence and liberality are both virtues of generosity that</u>
   <u>involve the spending of money. Magnificence involves a wealthy</u>
   <u>person spending a large amount of money, but liberality is</u>
   <u>being free with what you have, no matter how much. [4]</u>

15. Solomon was in many ways a virtuous king. Identify two of Aristotle's nine forms of virtue that Solomon can be said to share, and give a brief explanation of each. Which of the virtues did Solomon most lack?

   <u>Solomon was famous for wisdom, especially wisdom to administer</u>
   <u>justice. He was also magnificent, blessing all Israel with his</u>

wealth. However, he lacked temperance, giving himself over to physical pleasure. (Answers may vary) [5]

16. Consider this brief encomium: "Henry V was a great king. He ruled England with wisdom, defeated the French at the Battle of Agincourt, and sought to please God." Rewrite and improve this, including at least three of Aristotle's thirty noble deeds and two methods of improving the effect of praise. Hint: Keep in mind the St. Crispin's Day speech.

Henry V was one of the greatest kings of England. He ruled England with wisdom and prudence. He defeated the French at the Battle of Agincourt after winning many previous battles. He showed great courage by opposing a much larger foe in their homeland. Henry fought not for riches but for honor, believing that winning France was right for England. He did not surrender, but gained the victory, a victory unexpected given the circumstances. And he was a pious man, seeking God's will and pleasure in all that he did. For these things and more, King Henry V will always be remembered. (Answers may vary) [8]

EXAM FIVE

LESSONS 17-20

NAME

DATE

1. The three artistic modes of persuasion are ethos, pathos, and logos. Define *logos*.

   <u>Logos is persuasion achieved by the proofs contained in the</u>
   <u>speech. [2]</u>

2. What is the difference between special and general lines of argument? Which is more closely related to the study of formal logic?

   <u>Special lines of argument are based on propositions about</u>
   <u>particular subjects. General lines of argument have no</u>
   <u>particular subject matter but are applicable to all subjects.</u>
   <u>Formal logic teaches forms of reasoning well that are</u>
   <u>applicable to all subjects, and so it is more closely related to</u>
   <u>general lines of argument. [4]</u>

3. Complex terms can be divided into parts or into species. For the term *book*, identify three parts and three species.

   Parts

   <u>Pages</u>
   <u>Printed words</u>
   <u>Binding</u>

   Species

   <u>Reference book</u>
   <u>Novel</u>
   <u>Biography, etc. [6]</u>

4. Identify the five methods of defining terms. Define the term *vacation* using three of those methods.

   <u>Synonym: Holiday</u>
   <u>Example: Christmas break, summer trip to Hawaii, etc.</u>

Genus and difference: Leisure time away from regular work or
   study, especially involving travel

Etymology: From the Latin *vacationem*, "leisure, freedom from
   duty"

Biconditional: If it is a vacation, then it is liesure time away
   from regular work, and if it is leisure time away from
   regular work, especially if it involves travel, then it is a
   vacation. (Any three may be used) [8]

5. Name the three types of arguments based on the meaning of words.

   Argument by defining your terms, by considering the various
   senses of a word, and by modification of a key word [3]

Problems 6–7: Identify the quantity and quality of the simple statement, and translate it into categorical form. [4 each]

6. "Every farmer rises early."

   Quantity universal

   Quality affirmative

   Categorical form: all farmers are early risers

7. "Some birds cannot fly."

   Quantity particular

   Quality negative

   Categorical form: some birds are not flying creatures

Problems 8–12: Identify the compound statement as a *negation, conjunction, disjunction, conditional,* or *biconditional.* [1 each]

8. "All have sinned and fall short of the glory of God." conjunction

9. A man believes if and only if he is given faith. biconditional

10. "The kingdom of heaven is not of this world." _negation_

11. "To his own master he stands or falls." _disjunction_

12. "If we die with Christ, we shall be raised with Him." _conditional_

Problems 13–16: Refer to the statement given in problem 12.

13. What is the antecedent of the statement?

    We die with Christ. [2]

14. What is the consequent of the statement?

    We shall be raised with Him. [2]

15. Write out the conjunction that is the negation of the statement.

    We die with Christ but we shall not be raised with Him. [3]

16. Write a different but logically equivalent statement to the conditional in problem 12.

    If we shall not be raised with Christ, then we do not die with Him. [3]

17. Does the statement "All have sinned and fall short of the glory of God" imply that all men fall short of the glory of God? Explain your answer.

    Yes, because if the conjunction is true, then each part, including the second part given here, must be true. [3]

18. Write a statement consistent with but not independent of "To his own master he stands or falls."

    To his own master he stands. (Answers may vary) [2]

Problems 19–24: Consider the statement "No speeches are polemics."   *[2 each]*

19. Write the contradiction. <u>Some speeches are polemics.</u>

20. Write the contrary. <u>All speeches are polemics.</u>

21. Write the subaltern. <u>Some speeches are not polemics.</u>

22. Write the converse. <u>No polemics are speeches.</u>

23. Write the obverse. <u>All speeches are non-polemics.</u>

24. If "No speeches are polemics" is true, which of the statements of problems 19–23 must be true? (Answer using the question number.) <u>21, 22, 23</u> *[3]*

25. Consider the statement "All have sinned." State and explain two methods by which we may know this is a true statement.

    <u>We know this is true by faith in authority, since the Bible</u>
    <u>teaches it. We also know this is true by inductive reasoning,</u>
    <u>since we all have repeated experience with sin and sinners.</u> *[4]*

Problems 26–28: Circle the type of argument being used. *[1 each]*

26. "If you then, being evil, know how to give good gifts to your children, how much more will your Father who is in heaven give good things to those who ask Him!"

    Opposites   Correlative ideas   Rational correspondence   (A fortiori)

27. "If war is ever lawful, then peace is sometimes sinful."

    (Opposites)   Correlative ideas   Rational correspondence   A fortiori

28. "How can they believe in the one of whom they have not heard? And how can they hear without someone preaching to them?"

    Opposites   (Correlative ideas)   Rational correspondence   A fortiori

29. What is a *maxim*?

    <u>A maxim is a general statement about questions of practical</u>
    <u>conduct. [2]</u>

30. Explain the difference between a *paradoxical* maxim and a *disputable* maxim.

    <u>A paradoxical maxim seems to contradict itself or involve some</u>
    <u>logical absurdity, while disputable maxims seem to contradict</u>
    <u>some known truth or even another maxim. [2]</u>

1. What are the primary differences between *inductive* and *deductive* reasoning?

   <u>A good inductive argument makes a probable conclusion from</u>
   <u>repeated experience, while a good deductive argument makes</u>
   <u>a valid conclusion based on statements accepted as true. [4]</u>

   _____

   _____

2. What is a *fable*? <u>A fable is a short story that conveys a moral. [2]</u>

   _____

3. What is a *valid* argument? Include an example of a valid categorical syllogism.

   <u>In a valid argument, the premises imply the conclusion (if the</u>
   <u>premises are true, the conclusion must be true). For example,</u>
   <u>"Some syllogisms are categorical syllogisms, and all syllogisms</u>
   <u>are arguments. Therefore, some arguments are categorical</u>
   <u>syllogisms." [5]</u>

   _____

   _____

4. Rewrite and expand this argument from past fact in order to strengthen it, using at least two methods from the lesson: "Don't expect your house to be finished by the builder's estimated date. I have had two houses built, and both times construction was finished later than they projected."

   <u>You shouldn't expect your house to be finished by the builder's</u>
   <u>estimated date. I have had ten houses built, and all ten times</u>
   <u>construction was finished later than the builders projected.</u>

This was true for all of the different building companies I have hired, and it was true no matter what time of year the houses were being built. (Answers may vary.) [5]

5. Write an illustrative parallel to argue that you should not limit your reading to only modern books.

Limiting your reading to only modern books is like young people only taking advice from their peers. It ignores the wisdom of the aged. (Answers may vary) [3]

6. Write out the four rules of validity for categorical syllogisms.

1. If a syllogism has an affirmative conclusion, both premises must be affirmative.

2. If a syllogism has a negative conclusion, one premise must be negative and the other affirmative.

3. The middle term must be distributed in at least one of the premises.

4. If a term is distributed in the conclusion, it must also be distributed in the premise in which it appears. [2 each]

7. Write a sound categorical syllogism to establish this conclusion: "Some fruit is not a suitable ingredient in fruit salad."

    All tomatoes are fruit, but no tomatoes are a suitable
    ingredient in fruit salad. Therefore, some fruit is not a suitable
    ingredient in fruit salad. (Answers may vary) [3]

8. What is defined as "a syllogism with a statement left assumed"?

    An enthymeme. [1]

Problems 9–14: Write an argument of the stated type to establish the given conclusion. For problems 9 and 10, use the Aristotelian form "The fact that p is a sign that q." (Answers may vary)

9. *Complete proof:* "I have not yet completed this exam."

    The fact that I am only on question 9 out of 15 is a sign
    that I have not yet completed this test. [2]

10. *Refutable sign:* "The Apollo astronauts were heroes."

    The fact that the Apollo astronauts traveled a long distance
    is a sign that they were heroes. [2]

11. *Valid disjunctive syllogism:* "You should save some of your income."

    You either save some of your income or you have no money
    available for emergencies. You should have some money
    available for emergencies. Therefore you should save some of
    your income. [3]

12. *Valid pure hypothetical syllogism:* "If you dance regularly then you will live longer."

   If you dance regularly, then you will get regular exercise. If you get regular exercise, then you will live longer. Therefore, if you dance regularly, then you will live longer. [3]

13. *Modus ponens:* "Your passwords should be hard to remember."

   If passwords are to be secure, then they should be hard to remember. Your passwords should be secure. Therefore, your passwords should be hard to remember. [3]

14. *Modus tollens:* "You shouldn't believe everything you hear."

   If you believe everything you hear, then evil men will take advantage of you. You don't want evil men to take advantage of you. Therefore, you shouldn't believe everything you hear. [3]

15. Write a dilemma about whether or not to travel overseas.

   If you travel overseas, then you will spend a lot of money, but if you do not travel overseas, then you will not get to see the world. You either travel overseas, or you do not. Therefore, you will either spend a lot of money, or you will not get to see the world. [3]

1. Sometimes people speak falsehoods because they are *dishonest*, they know the truth and deny it. What are two other reasons people speak falsehoods? Give an example of a falsehood based on one of those two reasons.

   <u>People also speak falsehoods because they are uninformed or</u>
   <u>misinformed. For example, in Genesis 31, Jacob spoke falsely</u>
   <u>about taking Laban's gods because he was uninformed; he did</u>
   <u>not know that Rachel had taken them. [4]</u>

2. "It is right to lock up dangerous lunatics and criminals. Therefore it is not wrong to deprive people of their freedom." Refute this inductive argument by explaining where it fails.

   <u>The examples given here about lunatics and criminals are</u>
   <u>exceptions to the general rule. Despite these exceptions, it is</u>
   <u>still wrong to deprive ordinary law-abiding persons of their</u>
   <u>freedom. [3]</u>

Problems 3–5: Explain the rule (or rules) being broken in each of these invalid syllogisms. [2 each]

3. "No arguments are machines, so no arguments are things capable of breaking down, since all machines are things capable of breaking down."

   <u>The predicate term in the conclusion (things capable of</u>
   <u>breaking down) is distributed, but it is not distributed in the</u>
   <u>premise.</u>

_____

_____

4. "Some messages intended to be private are public messages, because some posts on social media are messages intended to be private, but all public messages are social media posts."

   <u>The middle term (social media posts) is not distributed in either</u>

   <u>premise.</u> _____

   _____

5. "Some medicines are not poisons, and some soporifics are not medicines. Thus, some soporifics are not poisons."

   <u>It has a negative conclusion, but both premises are negative.</u>

   _____

6. Write a counterexample to the syllogism in problem 5.

   <u>Some men are not physicians, and some surgeons are not men.</u>
   <u>Thus, some surgeons are not physicians. [3]</u> _____

   _____

Problems 7–14: Identify the hypothetical syllogism by writing the correct letter in the blank. [*1 each*]

A) Valid pure hypothetical	B) Invalid pure hypothetical
C) *Modus ponens*	D) *Modus tollens*
E) Affirming the consequent	F) Denying the antecedent

7. If you wash your dishes, then you are thoughtful. If you clean up after yourself, then you are thoughtful. So if you wash your dishes, then you clean up after yourself.   <u>B</u>

8. If my mother gets overwhelmed with happiness, then she cries. I saw my mother crying a few minutes ago. She must be overwhelmed with happiness.   <u>E</u>

9. If at first you don't succeed, then skydiving is not the sport for you. I never succeed in anything the first time. Therefore, I should not take up skydiving as a sport.   _C_

10. If I buy myself a car, then I will have to buy auto insurance. If I have to buy auto insurance, then I will need a job. Thus, if I buy myself a car, then I will need a job.   _A_

11. If a man is to succeed in Hollywood, then he must be able to act. Uncle John cannot act his way out of a paper bag. Therefore, Uncle John won't succeed in Hollywood.   _D_

12. If a nation plans to invade a foreign land, then they should build up their military. Canada does not plan to invade anyone. So they don't need to boost their military.   _F_

13. If you study for the exam, then you will stay up late. If you study for the exam, then you will get a better grade. Therefore, if you stay up late, then you will get a better grade.   _B_

14. I was told that if I take a trip to Honolulu, then I will enjoy my vacation. I really want to enjoy my vacation. Therefore, I simply must take a trip to Honolulu.   _E_

15. Refute this claim with a *reductio ad absurdum*: "No statement is completely true."

    You claim that no statement is completely true. But that claim is itself a statement. If you are right, then that claim is not completely true, and I don't need to believe you. And if you are wrong, then I don't need to believe you. If you're right then you're wrong, and if you're wrong then you're wrong. [4]

16. Consider this disjunctive syllogism: "Honors students can take either advanced math or advanced history. I opted to take advanced math. So I cannot take advanced history." Would this disjunctive syllogism be valid for the *inclusive or* or the *exclusive or*? Explain.

    <u>This would only be valid for the exclusive or, meaning you can</u>
    <u>take advanced math or advanced history, but not both. [3]</u>

17. Rebut the horns of this dilemma with a counter-dilemma: "If I maintain a Facebook page, then I waste time, but if I don't, then I can't stay in touch with my friends. I maintain a Facebook page or I don't, so I either waste time or I lose touch with my friends."

    <u>But if you maintain a Facebook page then you stay in touch</u>
    <u>with your friends, and if you don't then you won't waste a lot</u>
    <u>of time. You either maintain a Facebook page or not, so you</u>
    <u>either stay in touch with friends, or you won't spend time on</u>
    <u>Facebook. [3]</u>

Problems 18–25: Identify the informal fallacy being made. Be specific. [2 each]

18. My friends and neighbors all own big screen televisions, so it must be a good investment.

    <u>Ad populum</u>

19. Don't buy a big screen television. If you do, you'll start watching every football game, and then movies every night, and eventually you'll be glued to it and lose your job and your wife!

    <u>Slippery slope</u>

20. About a week after we brought home a big screen television, my son had a seizure at school. I blame the television manufacturer for selling me a dangerous product.

    Post hoc ergo propter hoc

21. I took a physics class at the university, but the professor was ugly, he didn't wear a suit, and he smelled bad. He must not know anything about physics.

    Ad hominem (abusive)

22. On the first day of physics class, we were taught Newton's laws of motion. But Newton lived in the seventeenth century, so his ideas are out of date and not worth studying.

    Chronological snobbery

23. I earned an A on the first physics test I took as a freshman. Clearly, getting a degree in science is going to be easy.

    Hasty generalization

24. Are you going to go on the hot-air balloon ride with me, or are you going to sit around and do nothing all day?

    Either-or

25. The first balloonists in France barely escaped arrest for trying to disobey the law of gravity.

    Equivocation

EXAM EIGHT

LESSONS 25-28

NAME

DATE

1. What is defined as "the adaptation of suitable words and sentences to the matter devised"? _Style [1]_

2. In two or three sentences, explain why it is helpful for a speaker to understand his audience.

   The speaker should understand the character of his hearers
   because different kinds of people will be persuaded by
   different kinds of arguments. We should adapt our arguments
   to our particular audience to be effective, but in a proper,
   nonmanipulative manner. [4]

3. Aristotle identified about twenty differences between young men and old men. List four.

Young	Old
Strong passions	Weaker passions
Look at the good side of things	More cynical about life
Trust others, having not been cheated	Distrust others, having been cheated
Courageous	Cowardly

   (See Lesson 25 for other acceptable answers.) [8]

4. Circle the nominalizations in this sentence, then rewrite the sentence, improving its clarity by turning some nominalizations into corresponding verbs or adjectives.

> Computers do not have the (capability) to experience (thought,) but they do have the (capability) for the (storage) and (processing) of data with extreme (quickness.)

Computers cannot think, but they can store and process data very quickly. [8]

5. Rewrite this grammatically passive sentence to make it grammatically active and clearer.

> A generous gift was given to the College of Music by the graduating seniors.

The graduating seniors gave a generous gift to the College of Music. [3]

6. Name the three levels of style, and circle the one which can be described in this way: "The purpose of this level is to teach or inform; stylistic devices are used, but are not apparent."

(simple,) middle, grand [4]

7. The lesson presented four methods of making your flow of thought clear in a series of sentences. Describe two of those methods.

Continue the next sentence with a subject that connects it to the previous sentence.

Enumerate key sentence in an argument.

Use transitional words and phrases.

Use the same word at the beginning of successive sentences.

(Any two) [4]

8. "A speech is a work of prose. Consequently, we do not need to consider rhythm in oratory." Correct this misunderstanding by briefly stating a proper approach to rhythm in speeches.

   Meter within a sentence is inescapable. The rhythm of prose is as present as the rhythm of poetry. We want our sentences to have a proper rhythm, without being overly rhythmical. The greatest orators use rhythm to make their speeches more elegant. [4]

9. Explain the difference between a *figure of speech* (scheme) and a *figure of thought* (trope).

   A figure of speech deviates from the arrangement or sounds of words, while a figure of thought deviates from the ordinary meanings of the words. [2]

10. What is an *allusion?*

    An allusion is an indirect reference, often a near quote, bringing something familiar to the mind of the audience. [3]

Problems 11–27: Identify the rhetorical figure used, by name, from the following list:

Alliteration	Dubitatio	Oxymoron
Anadiplosis	Ellipsis	Parallelism
Anaphora	Epanalepsis	Parenthesis
Antimetabole	Epistrophe	Personification
Antithesis	Hyperbole	Polyptoton
Apostrophe	Irony	Polysyndeton
Assonance	Isocolon	Rhetorical question
Asyndeton	Litotes	Simile
Chiasmus	Metaphor	Synecdoche
Climax	Metonymy	Zeugma [1 each]

11. "The search of science for the absolute weapon has reached fruition in this country. But she stands ready to proscribe and destroy this instrument." —Bernard Baruch, Speech to U.N. June 14, 1946

   personification

12. "I am the good shepherd." —John 10:11 metaphor

13. "We few, we happy few, we band of brothers." —Henry V, "St. Crispin's Day"

   anaphora

14. "…the pit is prepared, the fire is made ready, the furnace is now hot…" —Jonathan Edwards, "Sinners in the Hands of an Angry God"

   isocolon (parallelism)

15. "The highest duty of the writer, the composer, the artist is to remain true to himself…" —John F. Kennedy, "In Praise of Robert Frost"

   asyndeton

16. "…a frightful deluge of inextricable dangers, present disaster, and everlasting desolations." —Martin Luther, "Here I Stand"

   alliteration / climax

17. "This day shall gentle his condition: And gentlemen in England now a-bed..." —Henry V, "St. Crispin's Day"

    <u>polyptoton</u>

18. "You do nothing, you plan nothing, you think of nothing..." —Cicero, "Against Catiline"

    <u>epistrophe</u>

19. "Better is a dry morsel with quietness, than a house full of feasting with strife." —Proverbs 17:1

    <u>antithesis</u>

20. "...government...shall not take from the mouth of labor the bread it has earned." —Thomas Jefferson, Inaugural Address

    <u>synecdoche</u>

21. "The devils watch them... like greedy hungry lions that see their prey..." —Jonathan Edwards, "Sinners in the Hands of an Angry God"

    <u>simile</u>

22. "For they determine whether we use power or power uses us." —John F. Kennedy, "In Praise of Robert Frost"

    <u>antimetabole</u>

23. "Who shall give it to us? Shall it be imposed by chastisement, or shall it be freely accepted by penance?" —Fulton John Sheen, "The Cross and the Double Cross"

    <u>rhetorical question</u>

24. "When words are many, sin is not absent." —Proverbs 10:19, NIV

    <u>litotes</u>

25. "He blotted out every living thing...man and animals and creeping things and birds of the heavens." —Genesis 7:23, ESV

    <u>polysyndeton</u>

26. "…add to your faith virtue, to virtue knowledge, to knowledge self- control, to self-control perseverance, to perseverance godliness…" —2 Peter 1:5–6

   <u>anadiplosis</u>

27. "Look, the world has gone after Him!" —John 12:19

   <u>hyperbole</u>

EXAM NINE

LESSONS 29-30

NAME

DATE

1. How does the author of the *Ad Herennium* define *memory*?

   Memory is "the firm retention in the mind of the matter, words, and arrangement." [3]

2. How does the author of the *Ad Herennium* define *delivery*?

   Delivery is "the graceful regulation of voice, countenance, and gesture." [3]

3. What is *external* memory?

   External memory is information outside of our minds which can be used to recall what we need in a speech, such as notes, outlines, and books. [3]

4. Explain the difference between *natural* memory and *artificial* memory.

   Natural memory is the means by which we remember things without using special methods. Artificial memory is memory strengthened through special methods by which we improve our ability to recall things. [3]

5. One of the three levels of speech delivery based on the use of memory devices is using a complete script. Name the other two levels.

   <u>Partial notes and fully memorized. [2]</u>

6. Describe the repetition and removal method for memorizing written material.

   <u>Write out the written material, and read it aloud a few</u>
   <u>times. Then begin removing individual words or lines and read</u>
   <u>it again, mentally or verbally filling in the removed words.</u>
   <u>Continue this process until every word is removed and the</u>
   <u>entire portion can be recited from memory. [4]</u>

7. For the background and images method of memorizing, identify several of the properties of good *backgrounds*.

   <u>Backgrounds should be familiar physical locations (though</u>
   <u>not necessarily existing in real life). There should be several</u>
   <u>of them. They should not look the same, but should be</u>
   <u>distinguishable. They should follow an easily remembered order,</u>
   <u>such as walking a regular path through a house. [4]</u>

8. For the background and images method of memorizing, identify some of the properties of good *images*.

   <u>The images should be visually striking, strange, funny, or</u>
   <u>whatever will help the orator to easily recall the ideas or</u>
   <u>words. [3]</u>

9. What are the two most important parts of persuasive voice? Explain your answer.

The two most important parts of voice are volume and
enunciation. This is because a speaker's voice must be loud
enough and clear enough for his words to be heard and
understood. The other parts, tone and timing, are basically
useless if the audience is not able to hear what the speaker
is saying. [4]

10. In speech delivery, what is included in *countenance*?

Countenance includes general appearance, facial expressions,
and eye contact. [3]

11. Does *gesture* refer only to the movement of the hands? Explain your answer.

No, it also includes the movement of the head (such as
nodding), the shoulders (such as shrugging), and the rest of
the body. Even movement from one location to another can
be included under gesture, and should be considered by the
speaker. [3]